Division of Insular Affairs

Compilation of the organic provisions of the administration of justice in force in the Spanish colonial provinces

Translation

Division of Insular Affairs

Compilation of the organic provisions of the administration of justice in force in the Spanish colonial provinces
Translation

ISBN/EAN: 9783337154561

Printed in Europe, USA, Canada, Australia, Japan

Cover: Foto ©Suzi / pixelio.de

More available books at **www.hansebooks.com**

COMPILATION OF THE ORGANIC PROVISIONS OF THE ADMINISTRATION ·OF JUSTICE IN FORCE IN THE SPANISH COLONIAL PROVINCES,

AND

APPENDICES RELATING THERETO.

(1891.)

WAR DEPARTMENT,
DIVISION OF CUSTOMS AND INSULAR AFFAIRS.
July, 1899.

WASHINGTON:
GOVERNMENT PRINTING OFFICE.
1899.

INTRODUCTION.

The legislation relating to the personnel of the administration of justice in the colonies and to the organization of its courts is so extensive, so varying, and so contradictory, that a full review of the subject, no matter how succinctly made, would require much more space than the limits of the present volume permit. We have, therefore, been obliged to confine ourselves to some of the more essential laws, which may serve as a preparation to the study of the modern compilation.

The first source of the law appears in the compilation of laws of the Indies, which established numerous provisions referring to the various officials administering or assisting in the administration of justice; but as practical needs went on demonstrating the deficiency of this compilation, new partial provisions were published from time to time, some by the department of grace and justice, until 1851, when the colonial department (Ministerio de Ultramar) was created; the latter issued some more provisions; and not a few were decreed by the governors-general of our possessions, as well as by the regents of the audiencias. In this way a confusion of legal texts bearing on the matter was created, so that it is difficult to classify them systematically, as they are too numerous to be mentioned in full. For these reasons, we mention only the most important provisions, in their chronological order.

The royal instruction of June 20, 1776, given to the regents of the audiencias of the Indies, contained various rules on the administration and attributes of audiencias and the manner of filling vacancies; the *Real cédula* (royal letters patent) of February 27, 1796, approved the statutes of the association of court clerks (*colegio de escribanos*) of Habana, and another, of April 16, 1815, provided for the formation of the list of the *escribanos* (court clerks) to reside in Cuba; and the circular one of November 10, 1818, established the annual distribution of commissions among the *oidores* (judges who hear pleadings and decide suits in audiencias).

On June 19, 1831, a *Real cédula* established the audiencia of Puerto Rico and six mayoralties (*alcaldías mayores*), and approved the division of that island into judicial subdistricts; another *cédula* being published on January 29, 1833, ordering the fulfillment of the royal decree of the 18th of the same month re-establishing law 2, title 6, of partida 3,[1] which fixes the age of seventeen years as the minimum for practicing law.

---

[1] Partida 3. Part of a code of Spanish laws compiled by the direction of Alfonso X, called "Las Siete (seven) Partidas."

From among the measures promulgated in 1835 we shall only mention the *"carta acordada"*[1] of the supreme court, dated January 9, communicating the provisions of the royal decree of December 23, 1834, on administering the oath to regents, secretaries, and *fiscales* (public prosecutors); the Royal decree of January 27, communicating to the goverument of the Indies, for fulfillment, the *Real cédula* of November 27, 1832, which provided that admission to the bar (*colegios de abogados*) of the Kingdom should be open to all lawyers making application; the regulation of November 26 for offices of notaries public (*escribanias públicas*) of Habana; and finally, the orders published on December 20, 1835, for the audiencias in Spain were extended to the colonies, to be observed in so far as they did not conflict with colonial legislation.

On May 5, 1858, a royal decree approved the by-laws for the goverument of the bar in Cuba; the royal order of August 22, of the same year, extended to Cuba the royal decree of the 16th of the preceding June, creating an audiencia in the capital of the island, this audiencia being afterwards given the name of "pretorial" and considered superior in rank to the other territorial audiencias of our Antilles and possessions in the Philippines, and on September 26, 1839, the said audiencia was declared competent to appoint judges of inquiry (*jueces pesquisidores*).

In order to regulate representation in court, the regency of the Kingdom, by a decree of February 26, 1842, created two offices of solicitor (*procurador*) in every seat of a judicial subdistrict in Puerto Rico, issuing rules for filling the same and ordering the preparation of the corresponding regulations and schedules of fees; and in the next year the *auto accordado*[2] of October 5 approved the by-laws for the *Colegio de Escribanos* of Santiago de Cuba, in conformity with what was done in 1835 for those of Habana.

The state of disorganization of the mayoralties in the Philippines caused the publication of the *real cédula* of October 3, 1844, relating to the reform and reorganization of the judiciary in the said islands; while in the next year, among other less important measures, there were published the royal decree of February 25, approving the by-laws for the Association of Public Solicitors of Habana, and the royal decree of July 24, creating several mayoralties in the island of Cuba, and fixing the salaries for each of the three categories, viz, entrance, promotion, and final, into which the same were divided for this purpose.

Subsequently there were published the royal order of February 2, 1846, explaining the rules governing the seniority in service of the *oidores;* the *auto acordado* of the audiencia of Habana, dated April 19, 1847, establishing rules for discharging the office of solicitor; the *real*

---

[1] Carta acordada: Letter from a superior to an inferior court, with secret orders or instructions.

[2] A decision of the supreme court to be observed as a precedent.

cédula of June 27, of the same year, ordering the observance of the royal decree of the 24th of the same month, which organized the *alcaldías mayores* in Puerto Rico; the royal order of October 1, of the same year, ordering the formation of graded lists, fixing the seniority in service of judicial officials, which royal order was declared by another royal order of December 6, 1849, as not retroactive; the royal order of April 3, 1848, which provided that applications of associate justices and judges to contract marriage should be submitted with a report of the Governor-General and of the regent of the audiencia and presented with the consultative vote of the *Real acuerdo*, and the royal order of February 6, 1849, providing that audiencias should make report of the officials who did not return to their duties at the expiration of their leaves of absence.

In 1851 many provisions of great importance were published, such as the *Real cédula* of · January 20, ordering the enforcement of the royal decree of January 10, which established the precise conditions required to serve as advisors (*asesores*) to judges, and the forms and conditions necessary in filling vacancies in *alcaldías mayores*, according as to whether the places belonged to the entrance, promotion, or final category, and the royal decree of March 7, establishing rules governing applications for places in all the categories of the magistracy, the judiciary and the department of public prosecution in common law, and for suspensions, transfers, and retirement of the said officials, which decree established in its article 5 the various categories of the judiciary and of the department of public prosecution, and in article 9 the incompatibility of the same and ordered in article 12 the publication in the *Gaceta* of the decisions referring to the personnel, and in article 13 the formation of graded lists for all the categories.

Various provisions of interest were also published in 1854, of which the following are worthy of mention: The royal decree of January 27, reorganizing the *alcaldías mayores* in the Philippines; the royal decree of February 1, 1854, declaring the seniority in service, and precedence of the associate justices of the audiencia of Madrid and of the presidents of chambers of the other audiencias, who had been transferred as *oidores* to the pretorial one of Habana; the royal order of the 17th of the same month, ordering the application to Cuba of the regulations of October 14, 1852, as to the record of reports and on the manner of imposing correctional penalties on audiencias and inferior courts; the royal decree of March 15, creating in Cuba the offices of *abogados fiscales* [1] and abolishing the offices of agents of the department of public prosecution, and, finally, the royal order of July 31, on the substitution of *abogados fiscales* in cases of leaves of absence, vacancies, or sickness.

Notwithstanding this large number of provisions, great needs were noticeable in this important branch of legislation, and in order to fill

---

[1] *Abogado fiscal.* Official of the department of public prosecution next below in rank to *teniente fiscal.*

these needs and at the same time to uniform the precepts which had to be observed, a very important *Real cédula* was published on January 30, 1855, issued for the purpose of doing away with inveterate abuses and correcting illegal practices. It contained 12 chapters treating, respectively, of local judges, of ordinary subdistrict judges, of royal audiencias, of the supreme court of justice, of jurisdictions, and of special superior and inferior courts, of the powers of tribunals in matters of administration, of auxiliary offices and officials of the tribunals and judges, of the department of public prosecution, of challenges, of sentences, of appeals in nullity and cassation, and of liability and correctional penalties.

This *Real cédula*, which ceased to be in force first in Cuba and Puerto Rico and afterwards in the Philippines, was modified or supplemented by numerous provisions on the administration of justice in the colonies, of which the following may be mentioned: The royal order of the 1st of the following August, which extended to the colonial possessions the orders of August 29, 1843, November 14, 1853, and January 9, 1854, on the apparel and insignia of associate justices, judges, and officials of the department of public prosecution, and the royal order of August 19, 1855, establishing the judicial division of the island of Cuba.

In the period intervening between the last year above cited and the year 1875, when by the royal decree of April 12 a complete reorganization of colonial courts and tribunals was effected, the following measures, as of greater interest, deserve to be recorded: The royal order of January 17, 1857, increasing the salary of *promotores fiscales;* [1] that of March 30, 1858, creating the office of *secretario de acuerdos* [2] in the audiencias of Habana, Puerto Rico, and Manila, the duties of which had formerly been performed by the court notaries (*escribanos de cámara*); the orders issued in the same year by the regent of the first of the above-mentioned audiencias on the registry of rulings (*providencias*) and books of assignments and secret votes; the royal decree of October 1, increasing the personnel of the audiencia referred to above; the royal order of the 3d of the same month, ordering that associate justices discharge the duties of assistant auditor and, provisionally, the duties of auditor in case of vacancies; the royal order of the 3d of the following December, fixing the allowances of judicial reporters (*relatores*) in the Philippines; that of June 2, 1860, prescribing the number of public clerks' offices (*escribanías*) in Puerto Rico, and establishing rules for filling the same; the royal decree of the 9th of the following July, reorganizing the chambers of the audiencia of Puerto Rico and of the audiencia of chancery of Manila; that of the 30th of the same month, on the organization of mayoralties in the Philippines; that of July 4, 1861, on the powers of colonial audiencias; the royal order of the fol-

---

[1] *Promotor fiscal.* Official of the department of public prosecution, next below in rank to the *abogado fiscal.*

[2] *Secretario de acuerdos.* Secretaries of sessions *in banc* for the adoption of resolutions of general application.

lowing day, determining the personnel of the office of the *Secretario del Real Acuerdo* in the audiencia of Puerto Rico; that of October 1, fixing the salary of the employees in the office of the secretary of the audiencia of Habana; that of December 4, fixing the annual salary of regents of the colonial audiencias; and that of the 5th of the same month relating to the salaries to be paid to substitute *promotores fiscales.*

The royal order of March 20, 1862, regulated the granting in advance of leaves of absence to judicial officials and to those of the department of public prosecution in the colonies; another of the 4th of the following June, provided that court clerks should prove their efficiency before obtaining the office. On July 20 it was declared that the public department should communicate with the colonial department directly; on November 26, 1863, an allowance of daily salary was fixed for judges and other officials, when discharging their duties; the regulations of the peninsular audiencias, dated December 25, 1865, were extended to the colonial possessions; and many other measures were issued which are omitted here, in order not to prolong this review too far.

Subsequently to the important reform accomplished by the royal decree of April 12, 1875, there were published: the royal order of February 22, 1878, which abolished the chambers of war and navy of colonial audiencias; the royal decree of May 23, 1879, fixing the number and the categories of audiencias, as well as provisions for filling offices in the judiciary and in the department of public prosecution; that of November 24 of the same year, giving to the civil chambers of audiencias the cognizance of matters arising from the suppression of the courts of war and navy, and of questions of competency arising between ordinary and military courts; that of July 20, 1882, ordering the observance in Cuba and Puerto Rico of the law of civil cassation, which remained in force until the publication of the law on procedure of September 25, 1885; the royal decree of June 22, 1883, abolishing the general probate court (*juzgado general de bienes de difuntos*), which existed in the Philippines, and returning to the ordinary jurisdiction the cognizance of matters which had been heard by the suppressed court; an important royal decree of January 15, 1884, reorganizing the municipal courts in Cuba and Puerto Rico, and prescribing regulations for their operation; that of May 20, 1885, on appointment of judicial and of public prosecution officials, which fixed the conditions for entering upon either of these careers, and for filling vacancies; and another of the same date, organizing the personnel of the auxiliary officials of superior and inferior courts for a more perfect enforcement of the law of civil procedure in the Philippines.

The law of August 19, 1885, the principal object of which was to uniform the judicial and public prosecution careers in the Peninsula and in the colonies, before that time distinct and independent, determined the various categories, making them correspond with each other,

in order that the officials of the colonial possessions might be transferred and promoted to the Peninsula, and those of the Peninsula might
likewise be transferred and promoted to our Antilles and the Philippines. It provided that the conditions for entering on these careers in
the colonies should conform with the provisions of the royal decree of
September 20, 1875, although it extended to the said careers the articles
of the Additional Law of October 14, 1882, which establishes the order
of succession in case of vacancies. It further provided that the secretaries of grace and justice, and for the colonies, in accordance with the
orders of succession above referred to, and taking into consideration
the organization of the tribunals in their respective departments,
should fill vacancies which might occur with officials belonging to them,
being permitted, provided they fill the conditions established in the
said law, to appoint in the third or fourth rank those requesting a
transfer or promotion.

For promotion to the rank of associate justice of the supreme court
(*magistrado del tribunal supremo*), treated of in Article 50 of the additional law, it made the associate justices of the audiencia of Habana
equal to those of the audiencia of Madrid; it stipulated that in the
future there would not be conceded any uniformity of career to officials
of the department of grace and justice, and those of the direction of the
same name in the department of the colonies, although respecting
.privileges previously acquired by those who had already been declared
in the judicial or the public prosecution categories; and finally it
extended to the colonies the provisions regarding incompatibilities prescribed in the organic law, excepting the judges in the Philippines, who,
because of their office, in accordance with the laws there in force, would
perform, besides the judicial functions, other proper duties, as long as
the present organization in these islands should remain in force.

As a complement to the provisions of this law, the royal decree of
September 9 of the same year was issued prescribing that the orders
of succession established in the royal decree of the 29th of the preceding May for the appointment of judges of the promotion and other
categories superior to the latter, be subrogated to those established by
the additional law of 1882, and that the department of grace and justice
should formulate every year a single graded list of the judiciary
and of the public prosecution career, including the officials of the
Peninsula and of the colonies, in the order of seniority in their respective categories; for which purpose there should be forwarded to the
same by the department of the colonies, in the month of January of
each year, a list of officials of these colonial provinces, corrected to
December 31 of the preceding year. Subsequently the royal decree of
February 26, 1886, was issued creating the audiencia of Cebú, establishing the regulations for its organization, and fixing the limits of its
territory, and that of the audiencia of Manila; the royal decree of
December 26, of the same year, establishing rules for the preparation
of the graded lists; that of February 25, 1887, reorganizing the board

of codification for the colonial provinces; that of the 12th of the following August, extending to those provinces the law of June 18, 1870, for the exercise of the right of pardon; and that of July 6, 1888, establishing a board of revision for the proceedings of active officials of the administration of justice and for the collection of information concerning the ability of those who thenceforth should solicit reinstatement in the judicial career, and in that of public prosecution, which board was abolished by the royal decree of October 12, 1890; and the royal decree of July 10, 1888, ordering the publication in the *Gacetas* of Madrid, Habana, Puerto Rico, and Manila, of decisions concerning appointments, transfers, retirements with pensions, suspensions with salary (*cesantías*) of judicial officials, and those of the public presecution directly under the department of the colonies.

The important royal decree of October 26, 1888, the main object of which was the organization of the courts of Cuba and Puerto Rico, for the cognizance of criminal causes in oral and public trial and in single instance, introduced conspicuous changes in the organization of the courts of our Antilles, prescribing for this purpose provisions concerning the establishment of new criminal audiencias and the territory under their jurisdiction; the power and organization of criminal, superior, and inferior courts; the conditions for admission and promotion in the judicial career and that of public prosecution; order of seniority; titles and salaries of the officials; and the separation of the civil from the criminal jurisdiction in the courts of the capitals of Cuba and Puerto Rico, in conformity with the provisions established in the Peninsula by the royal decree of July 11, 1887, for those of Madrid and Barcelona.

This most important reform, inspired by a commendable intention to extend to the colonial provinces the oral and public trial with single instance before a collegiate court (*tribunal colegiado*), different from the secret examination system (*elemento instructor*), to thus facilitate a prompt participation of the accused in the preparatory steps of the real oral trial as a guaranty of its prompt conclusion, to place in the hands of the citizen legal means of a legitimate defense of what is closest and dearest to him and which should be most respected, to give to all an opportunity to assist to preserve public order, to respect innocence, and to punish crime, and, finally, to modify the penal procedure according to the principles admitted by science as indisputable—this reform, we repeat, could not have been extended to the Philippines because the backwardness of culture in these islands, the difference in language of their inhabitants, their lack of clear notions concerning public duties and those of citizenship, rendered impossible for the present the application of a system based on publicity of evidence and liability manfully accepted and understood beforehand, coupled with the duty to assist the administration of justice at any cost and without restrictions.

Another decree of the same date as the preceding one established the service of statistics of the administration of civil and criminal justice for the colonial provinces and possessions, on the same basis on which a similar legislation for the Peninsula had been promulgated in the decrees of March 18, 1884, and January 1, 1887. The royal decree of November 16, 1889, prescribed rules for filling the offices of court clerks in Cuba and Puerto Rico; the royal decree of the 28th of the following December established the rules to be observed for the appointment of substitute associate justices (*magistrados suplentes*); that of December 30 fixed the conditions regulating the filling of vacancies in the judicial and in the public prosecution careers, reestablishing for this purpose article 11 of the royal decree of May 29, 1885; and, finally, the royal decree of April 10, 1890, which follows this preface, charged the board on codification for the colonies with the drafting of a plan of judicial organization. The royal decree of the 13th of the following October reestablished the uniformity of the legal officials in the direction of grace and justice in the department of the colonies who were deprived of this right since the publication of the law of August 19, 1885; on October 13, 1890, a decree-law was published regarding the admission, transfer, and promotion of officials of the general administration of state in those provinces, many of which provisions, such as those relating to the time set for embarkation, allowance for transportation, and to other ones, are applicable to the officials of the administration of justice; and on the 31st of the same month the regulations for competitive examinations for appointments as candidates (*aspirantes*) to the judiciary were published.

The practical application of this accumulation of provisions, the mere enumeration of which is tiresome, was very difficult, and demonstrated the imperative and urgent necessity of compiling into a single set of laws all the precepts on the organization and government of courts. With this end in view, the Government first charged the committee on codes to draw up the proper project, and it subsequently inserted in article 25 of the colonial budget law for 1890–91 the necessary authorization to publish a compilation of regulations for the organization of courts, by virtue of which the one bearing the date of January 5, 1891, was published.

Neither the nature of this book nor its dimensions permit our making a sufficiently thorough study of the new compilation, for which reasons we confine ourselves to making some observations on the new legal text as briefly as possible.

It is immediately apparent that the greater part of its provisions are a literal copy of those in force in the Peninsula, and that where they have been departed from the principal deficiencies or imperfections are noticeable, as occurs, for instance, in the part referring to judicial irremovability, to which we shall refer later on.

It is also surprising that the authors of the compilation, instead of including in its precepts the provisions of the law of August 19, 1885, regarding the transfer of the officials of the colonial possessions to the Peninsula, a measure of so great importance, should have omitted the same in the compilation altogether; and that they likewise refrained from including the contents of the royal decrees of September 9, 1885, and December 26, 1886, referring to the formation of graded lists, and the royal decree of October 13, 1890, reestablishing the uniformity of the officials of the direction of grace and justice of the department of the colonies.

Leaving out the subjects comprised in the organic law, which modern principles of legislation consider a proper component of the laws relating to judicial prosecutions, the authors of the compilation have accepted the structure of the former and followed the method of the same with only the indispensable modifications in those subjects in which it differs from the standard according to which that of 1870 had been drafted.

The *promotores fiscales* and the present organization of the courts of first instance and of the justices of the peace in the Philippines are retained, as oral trial and the single instance for criminal matters, now in force in Spain, Cuba, and Puerto Rico, could not as yet be extended to those islands, for reasons apparent to all; and modifying in this particular the law of August 19, 1885, it gives the category of judges of entrance or of *promotores fiscales* of the promotion category to the vice-secretaries of criminal audiencias, who formerly were of a grade equal to that of *promotores fiscales* of the entrance category.

With regard to the substitute associate justices (*magistrados suplentes*), although it fixes the same requirements for obtaining appointments as are established in the additional law, this latter is departed from in the part in which the compilation provides, as did the organic law, that appointments shall be made for the judicial year instead of being of a permanent character, as they are in the first law cited, and in which it acknowledges the fitness for such places of the associate justices of local courts of administrative litigation.

In so far as one of the most important matters of organization is concerned, namely, that relating to admission and promotion in the career, the standard observed by the authors of the compilation is undoubtedly very strange; for, if their desire was that the officials of the colonies should be governed by the same provisions as those of the Peninsula, they should arrange them conveniently and insert them among the articles of the new set of laws, while the modifications which could be effected in the Peninsula in the future could easily be extended by Royal decree to the colonial possessions; and as this system was not adopted, the authors having limited themselves in this important question to so vague a declaration, it happens that, after the publication of the decree-law, there exists the greatest confusion concerning this point, and that the clear and explicit precepts of the Royal decree of October 26, 1888, have been substituted by many other provisions, in part contradictory and in part inapplicable to the officials of the colonies, as, for instance, the Royal decree of October 3, 1889, which gives to those serving in the Canary and the Balearic islands preference to being transferred to Spain, and article 23 of the budget law for the Peninsula, which concedes the right of entering as judges of the entrance category to secretaries and vice-secretaries suspended with pay, who may have filled these offices temporarily or permanently.

Some other provisions in force in the Peninsula, as those relating to promotions on account of absolute seniority in the career, and in their rank according to specified merits of those enumerated in article 170 of the organic law, it is impossible to presume whether they shall or shall not be applied in the colonies, as not even there have graded lists covering the whole service in the career been published, nor does the compilation prescribe anything relating to special merits for promotions. In any case, we believe that for their application to the colonies it will be necessary to publish some supplementary provision.

Regulations concerning announcements of competitive examinations for judicial positions, established by previous legislation, namely, by article 42 of the royal decree of October 26, 1888, were also modified in such a way that instead of being held annually, the examinations were held only when required by the needs of the service, the number of vacancies being taken into account.

Instead of following in the part relative to incompatibilities the accepted standard in what refers to admission, transfer, and promotion— that is, instead of declaring the laws in force in the Peninsula to be applicable to the colonies, the authors of the compilation have preferred to establish in a limited manner, and with great accuracy, provisions on such an important matter which, in the Peninsula, are the object of articles 117 and 120 of the organic law and article 29 of the additional law, of the royal decree of August 28, 1885, and of the royal orders of December 5, 1888, and February 14, 1889; the principal reform which the compilation contains in this point, and which has for some time been demanded for the Peninsula, being that of establishing that there is no incompatibility for an official in his native town, provided that his birth occurred during temporary residence of his mother and had so been declared, in order to avoid the really unjustified case of an official not being able to render services in the town of his birth, in view of his having resided there subsequently but a very short time.

The serious defects in the organization of municipal justice established in the law of 1870 having been made evident by long experience, it was to be hoped that the compilation would modify this law in the manner considered most adequate to its ends. Notwithstanding this and the reform which seems about to be realized in the Peninsula, the authors of the new set of laws, being inspired by the standard of strict uniformity, have limited themselves to copying the provisions of that law.

One of the fundamental principles of a good judicial organization, which was established in Spain for the first time by the royal order of October 16, 1840, and which was sanctioned in a categorical manner by the law of 1870, is that of the irremovability of judges and associate justices; and this principle, which has suffered many vicissitudes, up to the point of being annulled in practice, and which in obedience to the imperative demands of public opinion and convenience has been reestablished in all its force by the important Royal decree of September 24, 1889, is accepted by all as necessary for the independence of courts, because it constitutes the firmest guaranty of its impartiality and rectitude.

Notwithstanding this, the authors of the compilation, who have copied from the law of 1870 not only its structure but even the literal text of the greater part of its precepts, have ignored this guaranty; and without establishing this most important privilege of judges and associate justices, as was done in that law, they immediately take up in the corresponding title the subject of transfer, suspension, discharge, and retirement of said officials, introducing at the same time a reform objectionable in all respects, but which was a necessary consequence of the system adopted, namely, that of substituting the provisions of the organic law devoted to the determination of the just causes for the dismissal of judges and associate justices by others which treat of the discharge of the same, and which, owing to their vague and undetermined character, may give rise to the abuses of the discretionary power of ministers of justice.

We do not forget, in expressing ourselves in this way, the distinct political-administrative organization of our colonial provinces and possessions; rather, on the contrary, on account of these same circumstances; on account of the necessity to place the administration of justice on solid bases, which is the firmest guaranty of the respect of law and rights sanctioned thereby; on account of the advantage for public and private interests, in cases where the judicial officials are shielded from arbitrary decisions and abuses of the central or local power; on account of the fact that the same requirements for admission should be required as are in force in the Peninsula; on account of the grave injuries which are invariably occasioned by a transfer without cause, especially when such distant countries and such costly and troublesome voyages are in question, we are of the opinion that the establishment of judicial irremovability in the colonies was absolutely necessary.

Why has it not thus been done? This is a question we are unable to answer, as the authors of the compilation have not deemed it proper to state the reasons on which they have based their work.

Another reform, established since the royal decree of October 26, 1888, is the separation of the civil from the criminal jurisdiction in the inferior courts of Habana and San Juan de Puerto Rico, as was done in those of Madrid and Barcelona by the royal decree of July 11, 1887, and the consequent creation of the offices of secretaries of examining courts (*secretarios de instruccion*) for the courts of this name, all the court clerks (*escribanos*), as a consequence of this new organization, being assigned to the courts of first instance.

With regard to recording clerks (*escribanos de actuaciones*), although the purpose of the compilation is to extend to the Philippines the provisions established for those of Cuba and Puerto Rico, taking into account that they will be inapplicable in some cases, it prescribes the necessary rules in order that in such cases the clerkships be filled by persons of acknowledged fitness for the discharge of the duties thereof; and with regard to attending witnesses (*testigos de asistencia*), an institution peculiar to our possessions in the Philippines, in spite of being contrary to the principles of organization which the decree-law inspires, it has been necessary to retain them in the compilation because of the imperative necessity of not leaving without assistance all those courts in which there are no recording clerks as yet.

In treating of incompatibilities for practicing law, the compilation contains a precept which did not exist in the organic law, but which, however, is included in the decree-law, with relation to the employees of the colonies, namely, the one establishing that those who hold offices in the career of the general administration of State shall not be permitted to practice law.

This incompatibility, which neither exists in the Peninsula nor can be justified by any reason, far from appearing proper to us, appears objectionable in every respect, as instead of placing obstacles in the way of those who go to accept positions in the colonies they should be given every opportunity to increase their emoluments in a worthy and honorable way, as would be the practice of a profession which is not closely or even remotely related with the service of the general administration of the State.

We could make some other remarks, but we believe that those that have been stated are sufficient to give an idea about the new set of laws for the colonies, and the principal reforms which they effect.

It remains for us, before concluding, to repeat an opinion which is upheld by many, and which gains strength daily. If in the colonial territories there govern, with few exceptions, the same provisions as in the Peninsula as to the organization of courts, and the same substantive laws and laws of procedure; if the judicial and public prosecution careers of the colonies and the Peninsula are united, why does this branch of the administration not pass to the department of grace and justice, whence it originated, and from which it should never have been separated?

RAMON SÁNCHEZ DE OCAÑA.

JANUARY, 1891.

COLONIAL DEPARTMENT.

ROYAL ORDER.

As, the precepts regulating the organization of tribunals of justice in the colonial provinces are dispersed among different legal provisions, are deficient in some points not embraced within the limits and scope of those partial provisions, and furthermore are frequently hetero-geneous and often contradictory among themselves, owing their origin to distinct standards or responding to various exigencies of the moment, it is evidently advantageous, if not imperatively necessary, to gather and unify in one classified body all those which can be collected, har-monizing in the same all discrepancies which they contain, introducing such modifications as are suggested by the progress of science, the social evolution of those territories, the period of time which has elapsed, or which the lessons of experience may suggest, supplying the omissions that are noticeable in the scattered legislation in force, and forming, finally, a set of laws that would contain everything which refers to the organization and powers of those courts, while in the peninsula the law on judicial power, which is being prepared, is pub-lished and can be extended to the colonies with the indispensable modifications required by the special conditions of those countries.

Among the most important points which a set of laws of such a character should contain, the one which refers to the exact determina-tion of the independence of the judicial power, within the limits of its sphere of action, should particularly be borne in mind.

In order to maintain this independence the absolute irremovability of officials of the administration of justice is not necessary, a principle which, although formerly a dogma of certain schools, is at present an object of discussion and controversy among themselves, and the con-venience of its application very doubtful, provided it is replaced by such conditions of stability that said officials find themselves protected and guaranteed against possible arbitrary decisions of the ministers, without annulling the means of government which should be preserved by the central power.

Collaterally with the principle of the independence of the judicial power should be placed the bases and the rules which render efficacious the liability of the officials whom society entrusts with the sacred mission of administering justice. This point is one of those in which the legislative power should give in a short time enforced satisfaction, to the requirements of science and to the demands of public opinion, by

15

defining and regulating this liability, either in the law of the organization of the judicial power or by adopting wholly or partially the proposition which was submitted to the Senate by one of the most illustrious members of the Committee on Codes, over which Your Excellency so worthily presides. A problem of such importance should not in the meantime be left unnoticed, and if perfection can not be attained under present conditions, at least provisional solutions should be sought which approximate the same as much as possible.

The unification of the careers of the peninsula and the colonies being sanctioned by measures of a legislative character, the removal of all obstacles opposing this measure is of indisputable advisability for the practical realization of that useful provision, by facilitating to the colonial officials access to positions in the career in the Peninsula, if the former possess the qualifications required by law for filling these positions, and by creating at the same time incentives for those of the Peninsula to accept employment in the colonies, avoiding, however, the danger of converting these incentives into abusive means of securing rapid and unjustified promotions by leaving the present measure in force, prohibiting the admission of lawyers to the category of judges, based on the fact that the qualifications required by them do not offer sufficient guaranty of fitness for the discharge of the duties of such offices, and by determining the qualifications required of those who aspire to the fourth grades or ranks in the magistracy (*magistratura*), in order that the latter should not become an irregular means of obtaining employment in the Peninsula with fewer qualifications than are required by the laws in force.

As there is a university in Manila, which, notwithstanding the exceptional characteristics of its organizations, has a recognized official character, and confers academic degrees of the faculty of law equivalent in importance to those of the Peninsula and Habana, and the time being at hand when this university must lose its exceptional characteristics, and become equal in every respect to other universities of the State, justice, impartiality, and even political necessities advise the granting to natives of the archipelago admission to the judicial career, which is now to a certain extent closed to them, establishing the reasonable proportion of competitive examinations to be held in Manila.

The necessity of transfer from the Philippines to the Antilles, and *vice versa*, to which the officials of the colonial judicial career are compelled, in order not to renounce the legitimate promotions to which they are entitled in either of these groups of islands, constitutes for the same an irreparable damage, not so much on account of the trouble which such transfers cause, as on account of the many expenses disproportionate with the modest remuneration assigned to their offices. In order to remedy this evident evil, it would be desirable to investigate the advisability of establishing distinct careers for the Antilles and for the Philippines, without prejudice to the unity of the graded list, which at present exists.

If the supreme court is hierarchically superior to all other courts of the nation, both in the Peninsula and in the colonies, it would be advisable to have a chamber (*sala*) depending on the department of the colonies in the former, after the manner of the old chamber called the "Chamber of the Indies," which should be exclusively charged with all matters proceeding from these possessions; or, at least, if such reform is not feasible on account of financial considerations, it is reasonable that the secretary of the colonies should be entitled to appoint a just proportion of the vacancies of associate justices of that tribunal, in order to give a homogeneous character to the jurisprudence of the latter in reference to the special conditions of those countries, as well as in order to satisfy the legitimate aspirations of officials serving there.

The duties of judicial secretaries require habits acquired by practice, and conditions of stability which are at present lacking in the former, because their offices are included in the categories of the judicial career, to which they must pass in their respective succession; hence the necessity, which is imposed and which other considerations demand, of creating a special corps of judicial secretaries for all the grades of the administration of justice, from the municipal to the supreme court.

The establishment of rules for the substitution of judges, of associate justices, and of officials of the department of public prosecution, after investigation of the complaints arising on account of the system now in force in the colonies; the inclusion among the incompatibilities of that established by the law for the Indies, which prohibits the filling of offices in the career with persons whose relatives pursue in the same locality the profession of lawyer or solicitor, a preventive law the ignoring of which has been on more than one occasion a source of abuse rebuked by the public conscience; and the regulations for the transfer of personnel and for granting commissions, leaves, extensions, and dates of embarkation, the former being subjected to a system of guaranties against ministerial abuses, and the latter to conditions which would not permit arbitrary decisions and favoritism; all these are important points which can not be overlooked, some of which demand a deliberate study and a thoughtful solution. Finally, the regulations for the organization of the colonial courts, notwithstanding the provisional character which they must bear, must unite in themselves such conditions of foresight as are necessary to harmonize them, if not with the reforms which science prepares and reality reserves for the future, at least with the plan offered in the preamble of the royal decree of October 26, 1888, for local superior courts for judging minor offenses, with the institution of the jury in the Antilles which can not be delayed, and with the separation, in a short time, of civil and criminal jurisdiction in such localities of the Philippine Islands where the conditions permit it.

In view of the reasons stated above, it is the will of Her Majesty that the committee on codes for the colonies draft a project for the provisional organization of the courts of those provinces in which the above principles can be adopted, if a deliberate investigation of them demonstrates the advisability of their application.

I communicate this by royal order to Your Excellency, for your information and consequent effects, it being the will of Her Majesty that this order be published in the *Gaceta de Madrid* and in the official newspapers of the colonies.

May God guard Your Excellency many years.

BECERRA.

MADRID, *April 1, 1890.*

To the PRESIDENT OF THE COMMITTEE ON CODES OF THE COLONIES.

ORGANIC LAW FOR THE COLONIES.

COLONIAL DEPARTMENT.

ROYAL DECREE.

ARTICLE 1. The annexed compilation of the organic provisions for the administration of justice in the colonial provinces and possessions, drafted by the committee on codes of the colonies, is hereby approved.

ART. 2. This compilation shall be published in the *Gaceta de Madrid* and in the official *Gacetas* of the colonial provinces and possessions, with the character and force of law which was bestowed upon it by article 25 of the law of June 18, cited.

ART. 3. This legislative compilation shall become operative within twenty days from its respective promulgations, in accordance with the provisions of article 1 of the civil code.

ART. 4. The Government shall inform the Cortes of this decree and the compilation attached hereto.

Issued at the Palace on January 5, 1891.

MARÍA CRISTINA.

ANTONIO MARIA FABIÉ,
        Secretary of the Colonies.

21

COMPILATION OF THE ORGANIC PROVISIONS CONCERNING THE ADMINISTRATION OF JUSTICE IN THE COLONIAL PROVINCES AND POSSESSIONS.

TITLE I.

PERSONNEL AND ORGANIZATION OF INFERIOR AND SUPERIOR COURTS.

CHAPTER I.

JUDICIAL TERRITORIAL DIVISION AND INFERIOR AND SUPERIOR COURTS.

ARTICLE 1. The territory of the Spanish colonial provinces shall be divided for judicial purposes into districts (*distritos*), subdistricts (*partidos*), and municipal districts (*terminos municipales*), with the territorial audiencias, the criminal audiencias, the courts of first instance and examination, and the municipal courts or those of justices of the peace, which at present exist.

ISLAND OF CUBA.

Territorial audiencia of Habana.

PERSONNEL.

One presiding judge.
Two presiding judges of chambers.
Nine associate justices (*magistrados*).
One public prosecutor (*fiscal*).
One assistant public prosecutor (*teniente fiscal*).
Five deputy assistant public prosecutors (*abogados fiscales*).
One secretary of administration.
One secretary of chamber.

INFERIOR COURTS WHICH IT INCLUDES.

Examining courts...............	Eastern part of Habana (m–t).[1] Western part of Habana (m–t). Central part of Habana (m–t).
Courts of first instance............	Eastern part of Habana (m–t). Western part of Habana (m–t). Central part of Habana (m–t). Audiencia of Habana (m–t).

Bejucal (e).
Guanabacoa (e).

---

[1] The letters (e) (p) (f) placed after the name of a court denote that the courts belong, respectively, to the entrance (lowest), promotion (intermediate), or the final (highest) category; the letters (m–t) denote that the court is of the category of an associate justice of a territorial audiencia.

22

Güines (e).
Jaruco (e).
Marianao (e).
San Antonio de los Baños (e).

Territorial audiencia of Puerto Príncipe.

PERSONNEL.

One presiding judge.
One presiding judge of chamber.
Four associate justices.
One public prosecutor (*fiscal*).
One assistant public prosecutor (*teniente fiscal*).
One deputy assistant public prosecutor (*abogado fiscal*).
One secretary of administration.
One secretary of chamber.

INFERIOR COURTS WHICH IT INCLUDES.

Puerto Príncipe (f).
Morón (e).

Criminal audiencia of Matanzas.

PERSONNEL.

One presiding judge.
Two associate justices.
One public prosecutor (*fiscal*).
One assistant public prosecutor (*teniente fiscal*).
One secretary.
One vice-secretary.

INFERIOR COURTS WHICH IT INCLUDES.

Northern part of Matanzas (p).
Southern part of Matanzas (p).
Cárdenas (p).
Alfonso XII (e).
Colón (e).

Criminal audiencia of Pinar del Río.

PERSONNEL.

One presiding judge.
Two associate justices.
One public prosecutor (*fiscal*).
One assistant public prosecutor (*teniente fiscal*).
One secretary.
One vice-secretary.

24

Pinar del Río (p).
Guanajay (e).
Guane (e).
San Cristobal (e).

Criminal audiencia of Santa Clara

PERSONNEL.

One presiding judge.
Two associate justices.
One public prosecutor (*fiscal*).
One assistant public prosecutor (*teniente fiscal*).
One secretary.
One vice-secretary.

INFERIOR COURTS WHICH IT INCLUDES.

Santa Clara (p).
Cienfuegos (p).
Sagua la Grande (e).
San Juan de los Remedios (e).
Sancti Spiritus (e).
Trinidad (e).

Criminal audiencia of Santiago de Cuba.

PERSONNEL.

One presiding judge.
Two associate justices.
One public prosecutor (*fiscal*).
One assistant public prosecutor (*teniente fiscal*).
One secretary.
One vice-secretary.

INFERIOR COURTS WHICH IT INCLUDES.

Northern part of Santiago de Cuba (f).
Southern part of Santiago de Cuba (f).
Baracoa (e).
Bayamo (e).
Guantánamo (e).
Holguín (e).
Manzanillo (e).

ISLAND OF PUERTO RICO.

Territorial audiencia of San Juan de Puerto Rico.

PERSONNEL.

One presiding judge.
One president of chamber.

Four associate justices.
One public prosecutor (*fiscal*).
One assistant public prosecutor (*teniente fiscal*).
One deputy assistant public prosecutor (*abogado fiscal*).
One secretary of administration.

INFERIOR COURTS WHICH IT INCLUDES.

San Juan de Puerto Rico (examining) (f).
San Juan de Puerto Rico (first instance) (f).
Humacao (e).
Vega Baja (e).
Cayey (e).

Criminal audiencia of Ponce.

PERSONNEL.

One presiding judge.
Two associate justices.
One public prosecutor (*fiscal*).
One assistant public prosecutor (*teniente fiscal*).
One deputy assistant public prosecutor (*abogado fiscal*).
One secretary.

INFERIOR COURTS WHICH IT INCLUDES.

Ponce (f).
Coamo (e).
Guayama (e).

Criminal audiencia of Mayagüez.

PERSONNEL.

One presiding judge.
Two associate justices.
One public prosecutor (*fiscal*).
One assistant public prosecutor (*teniente fiscal*).
One deputy assistant public prosecutor (*abogado fiscal*).
One secretary.

INFERIOR COURTS WHICH IT INCLUDES.

Mayagüez (p).
Arecibo (p).
Aguadilla (e).
San German (e).

PHILIPPINE ISLANDS.

Territorial audiencia of Manila.

PERSONNEL.

One presiding judge.
Two presidents of chambers.

Eight associate justices.
One public prosecutor (*fiscal*).
One assistant public prosecutor (*teniente fiscal*).
Three deputy assistant public prosecutors (*abogados fiscales*).
One secretary of administration.
Two secretaries of chamber.

INFERIOR COURTS WHICH IT INCLUDES.

Binondo de Manila (f).
Intramuros de Manila (f).
Quiapo de Manila (f).
Tondo de Manila (f).
Albay (f).
Bantangas (f).
Bulacán (f).
Ilocos Norte (f).
Ilocos Sur (f).
Laguna (f).
Pangasinán (f).
Pampanga (f).
Bataan (p).
Camarines Norte (p).
Camarines Sur (p).
Nueva Ecija (p).
Tayabas (p).
Unión (p).
Zambales (p).
Mindoro (p).
Abra (e).
Cagayán (e).
Cavite (e).
La Isabela (c).
Islas Batanes (e).
Islas Marianas (e).
Nueva Vizcaya (e).
Tarlac (e).

Territorial audiencia of Cebú.

PERSONNEL.

One presiding judge.
One president of chamber.
Four associate justices.
One public prosecutor (*fiscal*).
One assistant public prosecutor (*teniente fiscal*).
One secretary of administration.
One secretary of chamber.

INFERIOR COURTS WHICH IT INCLUDES.

Cebú (p).

Ilo Ilo (p).

Antique (e).

Barotac Viejo (e).

Bohol (e).

Catamianes (e).

Cápiz (e).

Isla de Negros (e).

Leyte (e).

Misamis (e).

Samas (e).

Surigao (e).

Zamboanga (e).

ART. 2. The following are the grades of the judiciary in the colonies:

First. The presiding judge and presiding judges of chambers of the audiencia of Habana.

Second. The associate justices of the audiencia of Habana, and presiding judges of chambers of territorial audiencias.

Third. The associate justices of territorial audiencias, presiding judges of criminal audiencias, and judges in Habana.

Fourth. Associate justices of criminal audiencias.

Fifth. Judges of the final category.

Sixth. Judges of the promotion category.

Seventh. Judges of the entrance category.

The order of rank of officials of the department of public prosecution is as follows:

First. The public prosecutor (*fiscal*) of the audiencia of Habana.

Second. The assistant public prosecutor (*teniente fiscal*) of the audiencia of Habana and the public prosecutors (*fiscales*) of territorial audiencias.

Third. The public prosecutors (*fiscales*) of criminal audiencias.

Fourth. The assistant public prosecutors (*tenientes fiscales*) of territorial audiencias and deputy assistant public prosecutors (*abogados fiscales*) of the audiencia of Habana.

Fifth. The deputy assistant public prosecutors (*abogados fiscales*) of territorial audiencias and assistant public prosecutors (*tenientes fiscales*) of criminal audiencias.

Sixth. The deputy assistant public prosecutors (*abogados fiscales*) of criminal audiencias and deputy public prosecutors (*promotores fiscales*) of the final category in the Philippines.

Seventh. The deputy public prosecutors (*promotores fiscales*) of the promotion category in the Philippines.

Eighth. The deputy public prosecutors (*promotores fiscales*) of the entrance category in the same islands.

ART. 3. The first three offices in the careers of the judiciary and of the department of public prosecution correspond exactly with each other; the fourth of the judicial career corresponds with the fourth of the department of public prosecution and to the secretaryship of administration of the audiencia of Habana; the fifth with the fifth, and the secretaryship of chamber of the same audiencia; the sixth with the sixth, and to the secretaryships of chamber and administration of territorial audiencias; the seventh with the seventh, and to the secretaries and vice-secretaries of criminal audiencias, and to the secretaries of examining courts; and the eighth of the career of public prosecution has no equivalent in the judicial career.

CHAPTER II.

AUDIENCIAS AND INFERIOR COURTS.

ART. 4. There shall be in the island of Cuba six audiencias, which shall be situated in Habana, Puerto Príncipe, Santiago de Cuba, Santa Clara, Matanzas, and Pinar del Rio.

The first two shall be territorial audiencias and the rest criminal audiencias, the audiencia of Habana preserving its category of superior (de ascenso) with respect to all the other audiencas of the colonies.

ART. 5. Each audiencia shall exercise jurisdiction in the territory of the inferior courts which are assigned to it.

ART. 6. The audiencia of Habana shall be composed of one presiding judge, two presiding judges of chamber, nine associate justices, one *fiscal*, one *teniente fiscal*, five *abogados fiscales*, and two secretaries, one of administration and another of chamber.

ART. 7. There shall be in the capital three courts of first instance, to be called eastern, western, and central, and four examining courts, called eastern, western, central, and audiencia, with the category of associate justices of territorial audiencias.

ART. 8. In the territory of the same audiencia there shall be, besides, six courts of first instance and examination, situated in Bejucal, Guanabacoa, Güines, Jaruco, Marianao, and San Antonio de los Baños, all of the entrance category.

ART. 9. Each examining court of Habana shall have two judicial secretaries with the rank of judge of the entrance category.

ART. 10. The territorial audiencia of Puerto Principe shall be composed of one presiding judge, one presiding judge of chamber, four associate justices, one *fiscal*, one *teniente fiscal*, one *abogado fiscal*, one secretary of administration and another of chamber.

ART. 11. The said audiencia shall include one court of first instance and examination, to be situated in Puerto Príncipe and to be called after that town, and another in Morón; the former of the final category and the latter of the entrance category.

ART. 12. The criminal audiencia of Matanzas shall be composed of one presiding judge, two associate justices, one *fiscal*, one *teniente fiscal*, one secretary and one vice-secretary, and shall comprise the following five courts: North Matanzas, South Matanzas, Cárdenas, Alfonso XII, and Colón; the first three of the promotion category, and the last two of the entrance category.

ART. 13. The criminal audiencia of Pinar del Rio shall be composed of the same number and class of officials as the preceding one, and shall comprise four courts of first instance and examination, which shall be situated in Pinar del Rio, Guanajay, Guane, and San Cristobal; the first of these being of the promotion category and the rest of the entrance category.

ART. 14. The criminal audiencia of Santa Clara shall be composed of the same number and class of officials as the two preceding ones, and shall comprise six courts of first instance and examination, which shall be situated in Santa Clara, Cienfuegos, Sagua la Grande, San Juan de los Remedios, Sancti Spiritus, and Trinidad; the first two courts belonging to the promotion and the rest to the entrance category.

ART. 15. The criminal audiencia of Santiago de Cuba shall be composed of the same number and class of officials as the three preceding ones, and shall comprise seven courts of first instance and examination, which shall be situated, two in Santiago de Cuba, to be called northern and southern, Baracoa, Bayamo, Guantánamo, Holguín, and Manzanillo, the first two of the final and the rest of the entrance category.

ART. 16. In the island of Puerto Rico there shall be three audiencias—the territorial audiencia, which shall be situated in San Juan, and two criminal audiencias, one in Ponce and another in Mayagüez.

ART. 17. The first of the said audiencias shall be composed of one presiding judge, one presiding judge of chamber, four associate justices, one *fiscal*, one *teniente fiscal*, one *abogado fiscal*, and one secretary of administration, and shall comprise two inferior courts, one of first instance and another of examination, both situated in the capital of the island.

The latter shall have two judicial secretaries. The said audiencia shall comprise, besides, three inferior courts of first instance and examination of the entrance category, to be situated in Humacao, Vega Baja, and Cayey.

ART. 18. The criminal audiencia of Ponce shall be composed of one presiding judge, two associate justices, one *fiscal*, one *teniente fiscal*, one *abogado fiscal*, and one secretary. This audiencia shall comprise three courts of first instance and examination, situated in Ponce, Coamo, and Guayama, the first court belonging to the final and the other two to the entrance category.

ART. 19. The criminal audiencia of Mayagüez shall be composed of one presiding judge, two associate justices, one *fiscal*, one *teniente fiscal*, one *abogado fiscal*, and one secretary; and shall comprise four courts of first instance and examination, which shall be situated in Mayagüez, Arecibo, Aguadilla, and San Germán, the first two being of the promotion category and the last two of the entrance category.

ART. 20. The Philippines shall have two audiencias, both territorial, which shall be situated in Manila and in Cebú.

ART. 21. The audiencia of Manila shall be composed of one presiding judge, two presiding judges of chamber, eight associate justices, one *fiscal*, one *teniente fiscal*, three *abogados fiscales*, one secretary of administration, and two secretaries of chamber. This audiencia shall comprise four courts of first instance, in the capitals denominated Binondo, Intramuros, Quiapo, and Tondo; and besides, outside of the capital, those of Albay, Batangas, Bulacán, Ilocos Norte, Ilocos Sur, Laguna, Pangasinán, and Pampanga, of the final category; Bataan, Camarines Norte, Camarines Sur, Nueva Ecija, Tayabas, Unión, Zambales, and Mindoro, of the promotion category; and Abrá, Cagayén, Cavite, La Isabela, the Batanes Islands, Marianas Islands, Nueva Vizcaya, and Tarlac, of the entrance category.

ART. 22. The territorial audiencia of Cebú shall be composed of one presiding judge, one presiding judge of chamber, four associate justices, one *fiscal*, one *teniente fiscal*, one *abogado fiscal*, one secretary of administration, and another of chamber.

This audiencia shall comprise the courts of first instance of Cebú and Iloilo, of the promotion category; and Antique, Borotac Viejo, Bohol, Calamianes, Cápiz, Negros Island, Leyte, Misamis, Sámar, Surigao, and Zamboanga, of the entrance category.

The actual organization of inferior courts of first instance and of courts of justices of the peace in the Philippine Islands shall be preserved until the law of criminal procedure in force in the Peninsula and in the islands of Cuba and Puerto Rico is extended to the Philippines.

ART. 23. In each territorial audiencia there shall be a chamber of administration and those of justice designated in this decree law.

ART. 24. The chamber of administration shall be composed of the presiding judge, the presiding judges of chamber, and the *fiscal* of each audiencia.

ART. 25. In the audiencias of Habana and Manila there shall be two chambers of justice, one civil and the other criminal; and in the audiencias of Puerto Príncipe, Puerto Rico, and Cebú one chamber for both civil and criminal jurisdiction.

ART. 26. There shall be no other precedence among the associate justices composing the chambers of the audiencias than that corresponding to their offices and seniority.

The civil and criminal chambers shall aid each other in the transaction of the business of their respective competency whenever necessary.

Associate justices of either chamber, when not indispensable to form a quorum in their own chambers, shall act as substitutes for the associate justices of the other ones who may be absent or prevented from attending.

Whenever an accumulation of criminal causes in any audiencia renders such action necessary or convenient, a new chamber may be organized, which shall take the number following that of the last of the regularly organized chambers to assist the latter, provided there are enough associate justices for its organization.

ART. 27. The audiencias shall administer justice in the capital of the district.

ART. 28. In the absence of the presiding judge of the chamber, the senior associate justice of the same shall preside in his stead.

ART. 29. In accordance with the present judicial division the number of districts, subdistricts, and municipal districts can not be reduced or increased, nor can territory of one district be taken away from the same and added to another one, nor can the capital of a district or the seat of a subdistrict or municipal district be transferred to another place, except in accordance with the provisions of the next article.

ART. 30. Nor can any towns be separated from their subdistricts or municipal districts in order to be joined to other ones, nor reduce or increase the number of towns in which ordinary or extraordinary chambers of audiencias may be organized, except under the following circumstances and in accordance with the following rules:

1. That there exist reasons of public convenience sufficiently justified in the proceedings instituted in the colonial department.

2. That the municipal councils of the interested towns and the provincial deputation be given a hearing in said proceedings.

3. That the judges of first instance of the interested districts and the chamber of administration of the proper audiencia report on the utility, advantages, or disadvantages of the change.

4. That in no case towns be united in one subdistrict belonging to different provinces.

5. That the council of state be heard.

6. That it be resolved by the council of ministers.

ART. 31. The Royal decree establishing a change shall be countersigned by the secretary of the colonies.

CHAPTER III.

SUBSTITUTE JUDGES AND ASSOCIATE JUSTICES.

ART. 32. In each municipal court there shall be one substitute judge, who shall fill the place of the incumbent in cases of vacation, sickness, absence, incompatibility, challenge, or any other legitimate impediment of the incumbent.

ART. 33. Every municipal judge before taking possession of his office, or, at the most, within eight days following the one on which he shall have done so, shall propose three persons from whom one shall be elected as a substitute, stating the qualifications which determine his legal capacity and the respective preference among the persons proposed.

He shall submit this recommendation to the presiding judge of the audiencia through the judge of first instance of the district, who shall forward it with his report.

ART. 34. Substitute municipal judges shall be subject to all the provisions of this decree-law relating to the obligatory nature of the office, to the legal capacity necessary for obtaining the same, to its term, exemptions, incompatibilities, claims, and to the vacancies that may occur before the end of the ordinary term of their functions.

ART. 35. Whenever both the office of the municipal judge and that of his substitute become simultaneously vacant, or when on account of any of the causes mentioned in the law neither of them is able to discharge his duties, they shall be substituted by such persons as have held the office of municipal judge in the years immediately preceding, in inverse order, substitute judges, however, being excluded.

ART. 36. The municipal judges of the chief towns of districts if they be lawyers, and otherwise their substitutes who are such, shall substitute the judges of first instance and of examination.

No one possessing the qualifications mentioned above can excuse himself from the performance of the duties of substitute.

ART. 37. If neither the municipal judges nor their substitutes are lawyers, a report shall be made to the presiding judge of the audiencia, in order that he may appoint a lawyer to take charge of the court of first instance and of examination, the municipal judge in the meantime discharging his duties.

ART. 38. Municipal judges, who, not being lawyers, discharge temporarily the duties appertaining to courts of first instance or examination, shall employ lawyers as advisers in everything which is not of mere routine.

When this occurs the salary which would be due the municipal judge for his duties as examining judge or judge of first instance shall be used, as far as possible, for the payment of the fees which the judge's adviser earns.

ART. 39. While the municipal judge is discharging the duties of an examining judge or judge of first instance, his own duties shall be attended to by a substitute.

ART. 40. There shall be substitute associate justices in the audiencias, who shall be called upon to render services in chambers of justice, in cases when for accidental reasons the number of regular judges is insufficient to such an extent that the administration of justice would be delayed on that account.

Substitute associate justices shall be appointed by the Governor-General of the island, at the suggestion of the proper chambers of administration, and their appointment shall be made for the succeeding judicial year.

The number of persons selected can never exceed one-third of the number of associate justices assigned to the respective court.

ART. 41. The office of substitute associate justices of audiencias may be assigned only to the associate justices of the local courts of administrative litigation (*contencioso administrativo*), to persons who had been deans of the bar, or in default of both, to lawyers who may have practiced their profession for a long time, in a creditable manner, and paying the highest taxes.

The substitute associate justices, while attending a court, shall enjoy the same privileges and shall wear the same insignia as the regular associate justices.

Lawyers who have obtained said appointments shall have credited to them, in so far as passive rights are concerned, one-third of the time during which they have served as substitutes, or the greater time during which they really served; and if they practice the profession of attorney, they shall be considered in the same manner as though paying the highest quota of taxes, as long as they remain as substitute judges, in order that they may acquire the qualifications necessary to be appointed associate justices of criminal and territorial audiencias, or officials equal to them in the rank of lawyers.

TITLE II.

CONDITIONS NECESSARY FOR ADMISSION AND PROMOTION IN THE JUDICIARY, MAGISTRACY, AND DEPARTMENT OF PUBLIC PROSECUTION, AND COMMON AND SPECIAL CONDITIONS FOR THE VARIOUS JUDICIAL OFFICES.

CHAPTER I.

CONDITIONS NECESSARY FOR ADMISSION AND PROMOTION IN THE JUDICIARY, MAGISTRACY, AND DEPARTMENT OF PUBLIC PROSECUTION.

ART. 42. The entrance to the judiciary and to the department of public prosecution shall be according to the following categories:

1. Judges of the entrance category, deputy public prosecutors (*promotores fiscales*) of the promotion category, secretaries of examining courts, secretaries and vice-secretaries of criminal audiencias.

2. *Promotores fiscales* of the entrance category.

ART. 43. Admission in, promotion to, and filling vacancies of whatsoever category or class shall be effected in the manner and subject to the laws established, or which may in the future be established for the Peninsula, in so far as the special organization of courts in the colonial provinces does not conflict with the same.

ART. 44. In cases when competitive examinations are held, there shall be observed with reference to the same the provisions of the following articles:

ART. 45. The competitive examinations to fill the offices mentioned in article 42 shall be called when required by the needs of the service and for the vacancies existing at the time, including at the same time those in the judiciary and in the department of public prosecution.

If the number of vacancies does not reach fifty the call shall be made for this number at least.

ART. 46. The competitive examinations shall be held, whenever called for, in the Peninsula, Cuba, Puerto Rico, and the Philippines.

ART. 47. A call for competitive examinations shall be made by the secretary of the colonies, who shall forward the proper orders to the general direction of grace and justice of the department and to the respective governors-general of the colonial provinces, which shall be published in the official *Gacetas.*

ART. 48. In filling every 50 vacancies, 30 vacancies shall be awarded to the competitors of the Peninsula, 10 to the competitors of Cuba, 5 to the competitors of Puerto Rico, and 5 to those from the Philippines, distributing any higher number there may be in the same proportion.

ART. 49. The period allowed for filing petitions for admission to competitive examinations shall be forty-five days for those to be held in the Peninsula, and thirty days for those to be held in the Antilles or in the Philippines, counted from the day following the one on which the announcement of the examination was published in the respective official *Gacetas.*

ART. 50. In order to be admitted to the competitive examinations it is necessary to be a Spaniard, a layman, and a licentiate at law, graduated from a university conducted at the expense of the State, and to be 23 years of age before the day on which the examinations begin.

The following persons can not be admitted to the said examinations:

1. Those physically or mentally incapacitated.

2. Those who have been prosecuted for any crime.

3. Those who have been condemned to any correctional or corporal punishment.

4. Those who may have suffered and undergone a punishment which lowers them in the public esteem.

5. Those who have been subjected to a provisional suspension of proceedings (*sobreseimiento*) in a criminal cause, before this action has been converted into an acquittal by reason of lapse of time.

6. Bankrupts who have not been discharged.

7. Insolvents, until they are declared innocent.

8. Debtors to Government funds as taxpayers.

9. Those who have been guilty of acts or omissions which, though not punishable, lower them in the public esteem.

ART. 51. Those desiring to enter the judicial or the public prosecution careers shall prove the facts stated in the first part of the preceding article to the general direction of grace and justice, or to the respective governors-general, according as to whether the examinations are to be held in the Peninsula or in the colonies.

Proceedings shall be instituted for each candidate.

The lists of persons admitted to the competitive examinations shall be published in the respective official *Gacetas.*

ART. 52. The board of examiners for the competitive examinations to be held in the Peninsula shall consist of—

· The presiding judge of the supreme court, who shall act as the president of the said board.

The *Fiscal* of the supreme court.

Two associate justices of the same court or of the audiencia of Madrid, appointed by the secretary of the colonies.

The dean of the bar of Madrid.

A lawyer appointed by the secretary of the colonies, upon the recommendation of the bar, from among those who pay, as lawyers, one of the first three quotas of industrial subsidies.

A professor of law of the central university, appointed by the secretary of the colonies.

And one lawyer, as secretary, with the right to vote, appointed by the secretary of the colonies.

ART. 53. The board of examiners for examinations to be held in Cuba, Puerto Rico, or the Philippines, shall consist of:

The presiding judge of the audiencia of Habana, Puerto Rico, or Manila, who shall act as the president of the respective board.

The *Fiscal* of the corresponding audiencia.

An associate justice of audiencia, appointed by the respective Governor-General.

A professor of the university or institute, who shall be a lawyer, appointed by the Governor-General.

A counselor of administration, lawyer, or associate justice of the administrative court, appointed by the Governor-General.

A lawyer, appointed by the said Governor-General, on the recommendation of the bar.

A lawyer, as secretary, with the right to vote, appointed in the same manner.

ART. 54. The members of the board of examiners, who are not such ex officio, shall cease to exercise their duties when a new examination is held unless they are reappointed.

ART. 55. In case the presiding judge or the *Fiscal* of the supreme court, the presiding judge or the *Fiscal* of the audiencia, or the dean of the bar can not attend the board of examiners, on account of incompatibility or for any other reason whatsoever, they shall be substituted as follows:

The presiding judge of the supreme court or of the audiencia, by a presiding judge of chamber of the respective court, appointed by the department, or by the Governor-General, if proper.

The *Fiscal* of the supreme court and the *Fiscal* of an audiencia, by the *teniente fiscal* of the same court, and, in the latter's absence, by one of the *abogados fiscales*, appointed by the department, or by the respective Governor-General.

The dean of the bar, by a member of its administrative board, appointed in a similar manner.

ART. 56. The list of the competitors admitted to examination shall be forwarded, with the proceedings instituted, to the proper court.

ART. 57. On the same day on which a call for competitive examinations is published in the proper official newspaper, the appointment of the board which is to judge the same shall also be published.

The board shall draft a programme of the competitive examinations within the twenty days following said publication, giving preference to the civil, penal, commercial laws, and law on procedures, publishing it also in the official *Gaceta.*

ART. 58. Before an examination begins, competitors shall be numbered by drawing lots in public.

A competitor who, being called by the number drawn by lot, does not present himself shall be called a second time after the last number on the list, and if he again fails to appear, he shall lose all right to be examined.

ART. 59. The examinations shall be public; the first part shall be oral and the second part written.

ART. 60. The first part of an examination shall consist in answering, without previous preparation, ten questions, on subjects agreed upon by the board, and in the proportion designated by the same.

The time allowed for answering these questions shall not exceed an hour and a half.

ART. 61. The second part of the examination shall consist in the drafting of a sentence, decision, or complaint in a civil or criminal cause, which shall be decided by lot.

To prepare this work, the presidents of the boards shall ask the presiding judges of the respective audiencias for a number of sets of papers equal to twice the number of competitors.

These papers, arranged in such a manner that they shall conceal from view the work of which the exercises are to consist, shall be kept by the president of the board with the greatest care.

For drafting the decision, complaint, or sentence, of which the examination is to consist, competitors shall be kept separated in rooms for this purpose, and shall be allowed four hours of preparation, and shall have at their disposal the legal texts they may request.

After the four hours have passed the competitors shall deliver their work in an envelope, closed, sealed, and with their signatures on the outside; and when the board has convened, every competitor shall open his papers and read his work, afterwards leaving the papers in the hands of the president.

ART. 62. After the examinations of each day have been ended, the board shall immediately proceed in secret session to rate the competitors according to their merits by using one of the following two marks: *Passed* or *rejected*, and shall post the result of this action on the door of the building in which the examinations are held. When all the examinations have been finished, the board shall, in secret session, classify the competitors in correlative numerical order, submitting its recommendation to the secretary of the colonies.

Under no consideration shall the number of places announced for a competitive examination be increased; and the boards shall abstain from submitting in their recommendations a number of competitors greater than that of the positions for which the examinations have been held.

ART. 63. After the examinations have concluded, the lists and papers relating to the competitors shall be forwarded to the secretary of the colonies, those who have passed being named in the numerical order they bear in the lists drafted by the boards of examiners, and in accordance with the provisions of the following articles.

ART. 64. After the certification of the competitors who passed has been received by the department, the standing of the eligibles shall be drafted and published in the respective official *Gacetas*, subject to the following rules:

The list shall begin with the names of the competitors from the Peninsula, who shall be given the first three numbers; these shall be followed by the eligibles awarded number one in Cuba, Puerto Rico, and the Philippines, successively, the remainder of the list being numbered in the same proportion to the end.

ART. 65. Notwithstanding the provisions of Article 43, there shall be a preferred appointment, in which there shall be appointed as *promotores fiscales* of the entrance category those who have been suspended with salary of the same category in good standing, who may have requested the appointment.

ART. 66. Notwithstanding the provisions of article 43, there shall be an appointment by preference in which *promotores fiscales* of the entrance category of the greatest seniority, who have served one year in their office, shall be appointed to the positions of judges of the entrance category.

ART. 67. Positions of judges of the entrance category and similar ones and offices of *promotores fiscales*, which must be filled by competitive examinations, shall be distributed in the following manner: ¸

The former shall be given to the competitors who hold the first num bers on the graded list, in strict order; and the latter shall, in the same manner, be distributed among the remaining competitors who may have a right thereto, without prejudice in either case to the provisions of articles 43, 65, and 66 of this decree-law.

ART. 68. The competitors appointed to the Antilles, or to the Phil¹ pines, may either accept or refuse the office conferred upon them ur there occur vacancies in their category at one of the two places abr mentioned which they may prefer.

Those who are entitled to the position of *promotor fiscal* of the entrance category may likewise refuse or accept the same, until a vacancy of the category of judge of the entrance category occurs, for which, as in the preceding case, the competitor who has on the list a higher number shall be preferred to the one who has a lower number.

The right granted by this article shall terminate on the date on which the last position to be filled has been voluntarily accepted by the eligibles, it being understood that those appointed for the second time, in the proper order, who do not accept the offices to which they have been assigned, shall be considered as renouncing the career.

ART. 69. Officers who pass from one class to another shall preserve in the latter the seniority according to their category; and if they accept commissions for duties of a lower category they shall occupy the first place among the officers of the latter.

Appointments made for those going on a commission shall not deprive the appointees of their regular order of succession for appointments.

ART. 70. The colonial department shall keep the proper books of the personnel, with a suitable distribution of categories and series of succession, and an exact memorandum of the vacancies corresponding to each of them.

There shall likewise be kept the books concerning officers suspended with pay, in which there shall be entered the requests of those who desire to reenter the service, with discrimination between those who wish to serve in the Antilles or in the Philippines; and books of active officers who do not desire to be promoted outside of the Antilles or of the Philippines, where they are respectively on duty, and of lawyers who have already requested admission in the proper series of succession.

ART. 71. If in one or more series of succession there should be no officials with the legal ability necessary to discharge the duties of the office to be filled, said series of succession shall be considered as passed over and it shall thus appear in the respective books, the vacancy being filled from the following series of succession in their order.

ART. 72. The officials in the Antilles, to whom the series of promotion belongs in the Philippines, and vice versa, may have previously renounced such promotions by an official communication to this effect to the colonial department for the case in which by virtue of the same they would be obliged to pass from one of the above-mentioned places to another one; and the Government shall take into account said communication, if it deems it proper, when the respective series of succession is reached. This provision, however, is without prejudice to the right to transfer officers to any place whatever, from one point to another of the same category whenever considered advisable for the better service.

CHAPTER II.

CONDITIONS COMMON TO ALL JUDICIAL OFFICES.

ART. 73. In order to be a judge or an associate justice of whatsoever class or denomination, it is necessary:

1. To be a Spaniard and a layman.
2. To be twenty-five years of age.
3. Not to be included in any of the cases of incapacity or incompatibility established by this decree-law.
4. To possess the conditions established for each class of offices in the same.

ART. 74. No persons included in any of the cases enumerated in article 50 of this decree-law can be appointed judges or associate justices.

ART. 75. The offices of judges and associate justices shall be incompatible:

1. With the exercise of any other jurisdiction.

2. With other employments or offices endowed or recompensed by the State, provinces, or towns.

3. With the offices of provincial deputies, alcaldes, city magistrates (*regidores*), or any other provincial or municipal offices.

4. With subordinate employments in superior or inferior courts.

ART. 76. The discharge of judicial duties shall be a justifiable cause to exempt one's self from the obligatory offices mentioned in number 3 of the preceding article.

The authority whose duty it is to admit the exemption can not refuse it.

If anyone within eight days does not show cause for exemption from the said offices, it shall be construed that he has renounced the judicial position, which shall thereupon become vacant by law.

ART. 77. Those who are appointed as judges or as associate justices, while holding any employment or office of those mentioned in article 75, may exempt themselves from either of the offices or employments within the period of eight days following that of their appointment.

Should they not do so, it shall be construed that they have renounced the judicial office.

ART. 78. Persons related to each other within the fourth civil degree of consanguinity and the second degree of affinity can not serve as associate justices in the same court simultaneously.

This provision shall be applicable to the associate justices who are related in the degrees mentioned with the *fiscales, tenientes fiscales, abogados fiscales,* or auxiliary officers of the same court.

It shall also be applicable when the relationship within the same degrees is between municipal judges or justices of the peace and judges of first instance and examination with the *fiscales* of the same court, or of any court, with the associate justices of the respective audiencia.

ART. 79. In the cases mentioned in the preceding article, an appointment made of a person who has relatives with which the appointee is incompatible discharging judicial or public prosecution services, according to the provisions of the preceding article, shall be considered void.

CHAPTER III.

CONDITIONS COMMON TO EXAMINING JUDGES, JUDGES OF FIRST INSTANCE, AND ASSOCIATE JUSTICES.

ART. 80. No one can be an examining judge, judge of first instance, or associate justice of an audiencia, to the jurisdiction of which there belong:

1. The town where he or his wife was born, except in the case when declared to have been born during the temporary residence of the mother.

2. The town in which he or his wife has resided the five successive years previous to the appointment.

3. The town in which at the time of appointment he may pursue any industry, trade, or any remunerative occupation.

4. The town in which he, or his wife, or his or her relatives, in a direct or indirect line, within the fourth civil degree of consanguinity and the second degree of affinity, possess real estate, or pursue any industry, trade, or remunerative occupation.

5. The town in which he practiced law for the two years previous to his appointment.

6. The town in which he may have acted as auxiliary or subordinate officer of a superior or inferior court.

ART. 81. The provisions of the preceding article shall not apply to the offices of judges or associate justices serving in Habana.

ART. 82. The following officers can not pursue, either in their own behalf, or in behalf of their wives, or in the name of another person, any industry, trade, or remunerative occupation, or take part in commercial enterprises or corporations as joint partners or as managers, administrators, or advisors:

1. Examining judges or judges of first instance in the district over which their jurisdiction extends.

2. Associate justices of audiencias within the district over which their jurisdiction extends.

ART. 83. Those who violate the provisions of the preceding article shall be considered as renouncing the office they may hold.

CHAPTER IV.

SPECIAL CONDITIONS TO WHICH MUNICIPAL JUDGES OR JUSTICES OF THE PEACE ARE SUBJECT.

ART. 84. Municipal judges, justices of the peace, and their substitutes, must, besides the qualifications fixed by article 73, know how to read and write, and reside in the town in which they discharge their duties.

ART. 85. Wherever there are lawyers qualified for the offices of municipal judges, or justices of the peace, they shall be preferred for the said positions over others who are not such, provided there are no reasons advising the contrary.

TITLE III.

APPOINTMENTS, OATHS, AND ASSUMPTION OF OFFICE, SENIORITY AND PRECEDENCE, LIMITS AND EXTENSIONS OF THE TIME OF EMBARKATION AND TAKING PERSONAL POSSESSION OF OFFICE, HONORS, DRESS, AND SALARIES OF JUDICIAL OFFICIALS.

CHAPTER I.

APPOINTMENT OF MUNICIPAL JUDGES OR JUSTICES OF THE PEACE.

ART. 86. Municipal judges in the islands of Cuba and Puerto Rico, justices of the peace in the Philippines, and their respective substitutes, shall be appointed by the presiding judges of territorial audiencias on the recommendation in ternary made by judges of first instance of the subdistrict, during the first fifteen days of the month of May in the years in which renewal of appointments should be made.

ART. 87. In order to make their recommendation effective judges of first instance may, if they consider it necessary or advisable, request information of any judicial or administrative authority, or from any trustworthy persons.

No judicial or administrative authority can refuse to render assistance in the matter.

ART. 88. In their recommendation, judges of first instance shall state the circumstances which determine the legal fitness of the persons proposed and any other qualifications which recommend these persons for the office.

ART. 89. In towns which have more than one court of first instance, each judge shall recommend persons for the offices of municipal judges or justices of the peace, according as to whether judges of the Antilles or those of the Philippine Archipelago are in question, for that part of the town which is subject to their jurisdiction.

ART. 90. Presiding judges of audiencias may, when they consider it advisable, request information concerning the qualifications of the persons recommended, in the manner mentioned in article 87.

ART. 91. When presiding judges of audiencias find that the recommendations are executed in conformity with law, and if they do not make use of the privilege granted them in the preceding article, or if doing so, they are of the opinion that all the candidates proposed are fit for the position, they shall make the appointment within the first fifteen days of the month of June.

ART. 92. If one or more of the candidates proposed do not possess the legal fitness, while others do, the presiding judges of audiencias may make the appointment from among the qualified candidates, or they may order the ternary proposal completed by substituting for the candidates who are not qualified for the office those who have the legal qualifications.

When all of the persons proposed do not possess the legal fitness, the ternary recommendations shall be returned at once, so that they may be redrafted.

ART. 93: The appointments of municipal judges or justices of the peace shall be published in detail in the official *Gacetas* of Cuba, Puerto Rico, and the Philippines, respectively.

ART. 94. Municipal judges or justices of the peace elect who are disqualified from discharging the duties of the office, or are exempt from these duties, may request the presiding judge of the audiencia to declare their exemption.

This request shall be made through the judge of first instance of the district in which is situated the town for which the petitioners may have been appointed, within the eight days following the one on which they were notified of their appointment.

ART. 95. Those who are aware of any impediments that would prevent any appointee from performing the duties of a municipal judge or justice of the peace, shall state them to the presiding judge of the audiencia through the judge of first instance of the respective district within the period specified in the preceding article.

ART. 96. The judge of first instance shall forward as soon as possible to the presiding judge of the audiencia the requests and claims mentioned in the preceding articles, with the report he may deem proper.

ART. 97. The presiding judge of the audiencia, in view of the excuses or claims which may have been presented to him, hearing the public prosecutor and the chamber of administration whenever he deems this advisable, shall declare as may be proper:

1. The acceptance of the excuse or of the claim, in which case the appointment shall be void, and another shall be made.

2. The nonacceptance of the excuse or claim.

3. The verification and proof of the facts alleged or denounced. In the latter case the appointee shall not be given possession, if it has not yet been done until the case is decided; and if the appointee has already taken possession of his office, he shall continue to discharge the same until a decision is rendered.

ART. 98. Before July 15 the presiding judge of the audiencia shall decide all pending claims and shall order the publication in the respective official *Gaceta* of the corrections which have been finally made.

ART. 99. Those who have learned, after the municipal judges or justices of the peace have been appointed, that some of them are legally incapacitated to discharge their duties, may at any time inform the presiding judge of the audiencia to this effect, who, after gathering such information as he thinks necessary, and always a report of the judge of first instance of the district, and after hearing the opinion of the chamber of administration, he shall decide what may be proper.

ART. 100. Decisions admitting or overruling exceptions or claims shall always state the reasons.

ART. 101. From the decisions of presiding judges of the audiencias accepting or overruling allegations of exemptions or claims, an appeal may be taken only to the colonial department.

ART. 102. Vacancies occurring during the term of the two years fixed for municipal judges or justices of the peace to occupy their office shall be filled by the presiding judges of the audiencias, after the proceedings established in the preceding articles, in connection with the appointment, as well as in claims and exemptions, but without being subjected to the limits of time fixed in those articles.

ART. 103. Appointees for such vacancies shall cease to discharge their duties, if not reappointed, at the expiration of the term of the two years during which their predecessors should have discharged said duties.

ART. 104. The presiding judges of audiencias shall forward the appointments of municipal judges, or of justices of the peace, and their substitutes, to the judge of first instance, who shall inform the respective municipal courts or courts of justices of the peace, and also the appointees.

CHAPTER II.

APPOINTMENT OF JUDGES OF FIRST INSTANCE AND EXAMINATION, OF ASSOCIATE JUSTICES, AND OTHER JUDICIAL OFFICERS.

ART. 105. The appointments of judicial officers, from associate justices of criminal audiencias, inclusive, and up, shall be made by royal decree.

All other appointments shall be made by royal order.

In all the appointments included in this article the special conditions shall be stated by virtue of which the respective entrances and promotions take place.

ART. 106. Appointments of judicial officers of those newly admitted can not be made without previously instituting the proper proceedings which prove that the candidate possesses all the qualifications required by this decree-law, and the interested party shall make known by means of public and solemn documents all his qualifications for entering the career, and the special merits which commend him for the office and which may give him preference.

ART. 107. The Government shall report on the appointments of judicial officers to the proper Governor-General and to the presiding judge of the territorial audiencia, in order that the appointment may go into effect after the latter in a proper case informs the audiencia which receives oaths and gives or orders the possession of office to be given.

The Government shall likewise notify the appointees of their respective appointments.

ART. 108. The territorial audiencias *in banc* shall have the power to resolve upon the carrying out of appointments of judges and associate justices, and for this purpose the presiding judges shall order that all appointments be forwarded to the department of public prosecution for report.

When the report has been made by the department of public prosecution, an account of it shall be given to the proper court, which, if the appointment is found to be legal, shall order that it be carried into effect.

If the audiencias refuse to carry said appointment into effect, they shall respectfully submit to the Government the statement of the reasons for such action, and the Government, after hearing the full council of state, shall decide what may be proper in the council of secretaries. In the latter case the court shall obey the decision, without prejudice to the ministerial liability, if there be any ground for it.

Chapter III.

OATHS AND TAKING POSSESSION OF THE OFFICES OF JUDGES AND ASSOCIATE JUSTICES.

Art. 109. Municipal judges or justices of the peace shall take the customary oath, in order to take possession of their office, in the following manner:

Those of towns that are not seats of subdistricts before the judges who retire, or, in the absence of the latter, before their substitutes, at the place assigned for the sessions of the court.

Those of towns which are the seats of subdistricts and their substitutes, before the proper judge of first instance.

Art. 110. Municipal judges or justices of the peace and their substitutes in towns in which no judges of first instance reside, shall take possession of their offices at the time of taking their oaths; those of towns in which judges of first instance reside shall take possession of their offices after being sworn in, going for this purpose to the place assigned for the sessions of their courts and stating this in the proper memorandum.

Art. 111. Judges of first instance and examination and associate justices shall be sworn in, the former before the chamber of administration of the territorial audiencia to which the courts these judges have been appointed to appertain, and associate justices before the courts convened *in banc* and in a public session, attended by the representatives of the department of public prosecution and by all the subordinates and auxiliaries.

Art. 112. The form of oath to be taken by judicial officers shall be:

To observe and cause to be observed the constitution of the monarchy.

To be faithful to the King.

To administer strict, full, and impartial justice.

To fulfill all the laws and provisions relating to the discharge of their office.

Art. 113. Judicial officers shall take possession of their offices in the place assigned for their respective residences.

Art. 114. Judges of first instance and examination shall be installed by those who serve in the particular jurisdiction.

Associated justices, whatever their rank may be, shall take possession of the office immediately on taking oath.

Art. 115. During the act of swearing in and the installation of the presiding judges of the audiencias there shall be present the municipal judges or justices of the peace, and delegations from the bar, and from the associations of notaries and solicitors.

Chapter IV.

SENIORITY AND PRECEDENCE OF JUDICIAL OFFICERS.

Art. 116. Personal possession is that which entitles an incumbent to the pay and extra pay, as well as to the considerations attached to offices of the judicial career.

By personal possession is understood to be that granted by the respective chiefs and authorities.

ART. 117. Judicial officers who embark in the Peninsula or abroad or in any colonial province in order to sail directly to the place of their employment, shall enjoy from the date of embarkation, after the proper proof has been made, the personal salary of the class and office to which they may have been appointed, and shall acquire the seniority in the proper category, and all the other privileges appertaining to them in the capacity of colonial employes, provided that they take personal possession of their offices within the period specified in this decree-law.

In case of death during the voyage or passage or on arrival before taking personal possession of the office, the office shall be considered as taken possession of on the day of embarkation, with a right to all the resulting rights..

ART. 118. Of two officers embarking on the same date the senior one in the category shall be the one first appointed. If the appointments are of the same date the officer who takes personal possession of his office at an earlier date shall be considered the senior in the respective class, and in case of equality of conditions seniority shall be conceded to the one who shall have served a longer number of years in the next lower category.

If even in the latter respect the officers are on an equality, their respective seniority shall be determined on the basis of the period of their service in the judicial service or that of public prosecution.

In case these services are equal the oldest officer shall be considered the senior one.

ART. 119. Seniority shall give preference:

1. In the order of seats and positions among the judges and associate justices of the same class.

2. For temporarily presiding at chambers among the associate justices composing the same in cases of vacancies or any other impediment of the regular presiding judge.

3. For temporarily presiding in audiencias among the presiding judges of chambers in a case similar to that referred to in the preceding number.

4. In choosing one to attend the chamber of administration when one of the presiding judges who should compose it is absent, from among the associate justices forming the chamber of justice whose presiding judge may be absent.

CHAPTER V.

LIMIT OF TIME AND POSTPONEMENT OF EMBARKATION AND OF TAKING PERSONAL POSSESSION.

ART. 120. The periods within which embarkation of judicial officers designated for the colonies should take place shall be in accordance with the following rules:

1. Officers of recent entrance in the career who have to embark in

Europe shall certify by the respective captain of the port or consul that they have done so within the period of forty-five or sixty days, which can not be extended, counted from the date of the appointment, according as to whether they are destined for the Antilles or the Philippines, respectively.

2. Those who have been designated to an island different from that in which they reside or serve shall embark for their new destination within the period of thirty days, which may be increased by another equal period, which can not be extended, and which will be granted at the discretion of the proper Governor-General, the special circumstances of each case being taken into account. The first period referred to shall be computed from the day following that on which approval was made of the order which gave rise to the embarkation.

The officers referred to in the preceding paragraph may remain in the Peninsula for the periods specified in article 126 of this decree-law.

ART. 121. When the lack of means of communication absolutely prevents the fulfillment of the provisions of this decree-law referring to periods of embarkation and taking personal possession of offices, the Governor-General shall assign the period which he considers necessary, according to the circumstances, in order that the officers may be able to report for duty.

ART. 122. In the copies of appointments made by the colonial department the period for embarkation shall always be fixed in accordance with rule 1 of article 120.

ART. 123. Notwithstanding the provisions of the preceding articles, the appointees may be obliged to embark within any other periods shorter than those fixed, if special circumstances so require.

The preceding precept may likewise be applied to the periods allowed for taking personal possession of office.

ART. 124. A promoted or transferred employe, who is retired within the period of presentation, shall receive the salary of the office previously occupied until the date on which he is declared suspended with pay or pensioned.

ART. 125. Judicial officers shall take personal possession of their offices within the period of thirty days following the one cn which the royal command is approved, or the date on which the officer has landed on the island to which he is appointed, according as to whether the appointees come from the same island to which they are assigned or not.

The period specified in this article may be extended by another period of an equal length, which can not be extended, and which shall be granted at the discretion of the proper Governor-General, when there are grounds sufficiently justified for such action.

ART. 126. Officers transferred from the Philippines to the Antilles, or vice versa, may remain in Europe thirty days, computed from the day of their landing, with the right to the salary of their new office from the date of their departure from the point of the residence of the one they previously held, provided that they take possession of the former.

If, however, this period has elapsed, and the officer does not continue his journey, it shall be construed that he renounces the service, except when the Government authorizes him to stay thirty days longer, such action being based on the fact that the officer could not embark on account of sickness or any other cause duly proved, in which case the officer shall continue to draw the personal salary.

ART. 127. If officers have exceeded the periods of time allowed them in the respective cases fixed in this chapter, their appointments shall become void, and said officers shall be declared suspended, with pay, when such action is proper, and in this case new appointments may be given them, when opportunity offers, in the series of succession of officers suspended with pay.

CHAPTER VI.

HONORS OF JUDGES AND ASSOCIATE JUSTICES.

ART. 128. Courts shall be addressed orally and in writing by imper- sonal titles (*tratamiento impersonal*).

ART. 129. Examining and first instance judges shall have in official actions the title of *Señoria*

ART. 130. Associate justices and presiding judges of chambers of audiencias shall have the personal title of *Señoria*.

ART. 131. Presiding judges of territorial audiencias and those of chambers of Habana shall be given the title of *Señoria ilustrisima*.

ART. 132. In official actions judges and associate justices shall not be given a greater title than that which belongs to their actual office in the judicial career, although they may have a higher title in a different career, or on account of other titles.

Neither shall they use, while assembling in body or in chambers, any decorations which gives them right to a title higher than that which belongs to the presiding officer.

ART. 133. Judges and associate justices who have been pensioned or have voluntarily retired from the service, or because of impossibility to serve longer, shall preserve the personal title obtained in the service, and those who have been removed from office, shall lose them in the cases and in the form prescribed by this decree-law.

ART. 134. Notwithstanding the provisions of the preceding article, pensioned judges and associate justices who have been in the actual judicial service for more than twenty-five years may obtain the honors of the category next above that of their last office, if they deserve such reward, for numerous and distinguished services in the said career.

ART. 135. With the exception of the case stated in the preceding article, titles due judges and associate justices shall not be granted, nor shall those who are judges and associate justices be given a rank higher than that belonging to the office they hold.

ART. 136. Municipal judges and their substitutes, when they replace the former, shall, in all the acts in which they exercise jurisdiction or convene as such, wear the insignia proper to their office.

ART. 137. Judges and associate justices during public sessions, in other official acts inside the building, and in the solemn acts in which they assemble in committee or in body, in conformity with this decree, or whenever ordered to do so by royal order, shall wear ceremonial dress.

ART. 138. Ceremonial dress shall be:

For examining and first instance judges the gown, medal, and badge which are prescribed for them by the provisions in force.

For associate justices of audiencias the prescribed gown, medal, and badge.

In the remaining official acts not mentioned in the preceding article, judges and associate justices shall use only the badge or medal and the cane, with distinctive sign which is assigned them.

ART. 139. No judge or associate justice can wear other dress or other insignia than those proper to their office in the judicial service, nor decorations higher than those worn by the presiding judge.

CHAPTER VIII.

PAY OF JUDICIAL OFFICERS.

ART. 140. Municipal judges or justices of the peace, and their substitutes, shall receive only the fees fixed by the schedules of judicial fees.

ART. 141. Judges of first instance of the entrance category, and the other officers of the same rank, shall receive 750 pesos of pay and 1,125 pesos of extra pay.

Judges of first instance of the promotion category and other officers of equal rank, 900 pesos of pay and 1,350 pesos of extra pay.

Judges of the final category and other officers of equal rank, 1,100 pesos of pay, and 1,650 pesos of extra pay.

The associate justices of criminal audiencias and other officers of the same rank, 1,400 pesos of pay and 2,100 pesos of extra pay.

The associate justices of territorial audiencias and other officers of the same rank, 1,700 pesos of pay and 2,550 of extra pay.

The associate justices of the audiencia of Habana and other officers of the same rank, 2,000 pesos of pay and 3,000 pesos of extra pay.

The presiding judge and presiding judges of chamber of the audiencia of Habana, 2,300 pesos of pay and 3,450 of extra pay.

ART. 142. The associate justices and the auxiliary and subordinate officers of audiencias, when leaving the place of residence of the same in order to convene in a chamber of justice, shall receive the following daily allowances:

Associate justices, 6 pesos per day; secretaries, 3 pesos; court officers and doorkeepers, 1 peso. This increase of salary shall not be taken into account in the payment of pensions.

ART. 143. No substitute shall get a salary other than that of his regular office.

Offices which can not be substituted according to regulations, shall be intrusted to active officers or those suspended with pay, and private persons as temporary appointees, when such action is demanded by the requirements of the service.

In such cases, no matter whether the position which is thus occupied is the first vacancy occurring, or one caused or produced by other vacancies, the interested parties shall receive either the pay only, or both the pay and extra pay fixed in the budget for the duties intrusted to them, according as to whether the vacancy is accidental or absolute.

ART. 144. All temporary occupation of offices of royal appointment shall be submitted to the approval of the Colonial Department.

ART. 145. The time of temporary service rendered by officers suspended with pay shall be credited for their classification on the passive list, provided that their temporary employment was approved by royal order.

ART. 146. All officers in the judicial service or in that of public prosecution shall have a right to allowance for transportation expenses, in the manner and under the conditions established by the legislation in force on the subject.

TITLE IV.

TRANSFERS, SUSPENSION, RETIREMENT, REMOVAL, AND PENSIONING OF JUDICIAL OFFICERS.

CHAPTER I.

TRANSFERS.

ART. 147. Judicial officers, with the exception of those serving in Habana, must necessarily be transferred:

1. When they have resided in the same town for eight years.

2. When by the acts of another party, and not by his own, any one of the former, his wife, or his or her ascendants or descendants, or collateral relations within the fourth degree of cousanguinity or second degree of affinity, acquired real estate within the territory over which the jurisdiction of the superior or inferior court to which he belongs extends.

3. If on account of any circumstance which is not the one specified in article 152 there happen to be in the same court or audiencia two persons related to each other within the fourth degree of consanguinity

or second of affinity, in which case the Government shall see that the transfer takes place within four months.

4. In the cases mentioned in article 152 the transfer shall be made, whenever possible, within one year from the date on which the suspension began.

ART. 148. Judicial officers may be transferred:

1. On account of serious disagreements with the other members of the court to which they belong.

2. When the chamber of administration of an audiencia, for well-founded reasons, recommends the transfer of judges, secretaries, and vice-secretaries, or that of the supreme court the transfer of associate justices.

3. When circumstances of some other kind, or very important considerations of public order, require such transfers.

<h2 style="text-align:center">CHAPTER II.</h2>

<h3 style="text-align:center">SUSPENSIONS.</h3>

ART. 149. Suspensions of judicial officers shall take place by a decision of the competent court in the following cases:

1. When it has been declared that there are grounds for criminal prosecution against the same for crimes committed in the exercise of their duties.

2. When for any other crime they have been sentenced to imprisonment or to an equivalent bond.

3. If, without previous imprisonment or bond, either corporeal or correctional punishment of the same has been demanded by the department of public prosecution.

4. When they have received any disciplinary punishment for serious acts which, without constituting crimes, compromise the dignity of their office and lower them in the public esteem.

5. When the suspension is decreed by way of discipline.

Presiding judges of territorial audiencias, on their own responsibility, and hearing the chamber of administration, may also suspend an examining or first-instance judge, after proceedings in which there appears a request of suspension by the Governor-General or by the hierarchical superior of the person concerned, or for any other sufficient grounds in his judgment.

The proceedings shall immediately be forwarded with his report to the Government.

In this case one of the following three decisions is possible:

1. Removal of the suspension.

2. Transfer of the person interested.

3. Decision of dismissal.

In the latter case the prescriptions of article 156 shall be observed.

ART. 150. In the first three cases of the preceding article the court having cognizance of the cause shall order the suspension in the same decree which sets forth the ruling therefor.

In the fourth case the chamber of administration of the proper audiencia shall order the suspension of judges, secretaries, and vice-secretaries; and the chamber of administration of the supreme court of associate justices. For this purpose they shall resolve themselves into chambers of justice and shall call up the facts relating to the penalties imposed.

In the fifth case the penalty shall be imposed by the court or the chamber of administration to which the cognizance of the offense that gives rise to the disciplinary penalty belongs, convening for the purpose as a chamber of justice.

In the last two cases the officer concerned shall be given a hearing either in writing or orally, if he appears on summons issued to him.

ART. 151. The suspension shall last:

In cases 1, 2, and 3 of article 149, until a sentence of acquittal has been pronounced or a suspension of proceedings has been decided upon.

In case 4, until an acquittal has been declared or refused.

In case 5, during the whole period fixed in the sentence of disciplinary penalty.

ART. 152. A disciplinary suspension of judicial officers, with the exception of those serving in Habana, until they are transferrred to other points, shall be proper in the following cases:

1. When they marry a woman born within the subdistrict (partido), district (distrito), or municipal district in which they discharge their duties, except when the birth has been declared as having taken place during the temporary residence of the mother, by the Colonial Department; or when they marry a woman who resides or owns real estate in the localities in question, or when real estate in those localities is owned by her relatives in a direct ascending or descending line, or collateral relatives to the second degree.

2. When by their own acts, or by the acts of their wives, they have acquired real property in the said territory; but not when they have acquired said property by inheritance or by the acts of a third party.

ART. 153. The suspension in the cases specified in the preceding article shall be decreed by the chamber of administration of the supreme court when associate justices are involved, and by the chambers of administration of audiencias when other judicial officers are concerned.

In both cases they shall convene for the purpose as chambers of justice, shall summon the persons interested, and, if they appear, shall give them a hearing in writing or orally.

ART. 154. In cases 1, 2, and 3 of article 149 the suspended officer shall draw one-half of his salary.

In cases 4 and 5 of the same article and in those specified in article 152 he shall not draw any salary at all.

ART. 155. When the suspended officer is acquitted in cases 1, 2, and 3 of article 149 he shall be credited the part of his salary which he may not have drawn during his suspension.

CHAPTER III.

DISMISSALS.

ART. 156. Dismissals shall be made when, in the opinion of the Government, the officer concerned takes part in political affairs other than casting his electoral vote.

In every case proceedings shall be instituted, in which shall be heard the Governor-General and the respective presiding judge and *fiscal.*

If an associate justice is involved, the chamber of administration of the supreme court shall also be heard.

The person interested shall always be given a hearing; who shall have, besides, a right to the concession of a reasonable time necessary for his defense.

Until an officer has been personally notified of his dismissal the steps taken against him shall be considered as a mere suspension.

CHAPTER IV.

RETIREMENT WITH PENSION.

ART. 157. Judicial officers who are physically or mentally incapacitated for the service shall be retired with pension.

ART. 158. The following officers may be retired with pension on their request or by the decision of the Government:

Associate justices who have reached the age of 70 years.

Other officers who have reached the age of 65.

ART. 159. When a retirement with pension is not made at the request of the person interested a hearing must be given to the said officer in the administrative proceedings instituted for the purpose, if based on the causes specified in article 157.

ART. 160. Judicial officers shall have at their retirement the pay to which they are entitled according to their years of service, in the same terms as those who draw an equal salary in the other careers of the State, adding to the same the increase of eight years which corresponds to them by virtue of the career.

ART. 161. Officers retired with pension on account of incapacity caused by injuries received in the acts of service or as a consequence of the service shall enjoy:

The full salary which they drew in active service, if they had served for twenty years in the judicial or public prosecution careers.

Four-fifths of the said salary, no matter what may be the number of years of their service.

ART. 162. Officers who are retired with pension on account of incapacity before reaching 60 years may be reinstated and return to the service, proving that the cause for the retirement has disappeared, and after the council of State has been heard.

Reinstated officers shall continue to draw the salary belonging to them as retired officers with pension until they are given a new position.

TITLE V.

JUDICIAL LIABILITY

CHAPTER I.

CRIMINAL LIABILITY OF JUDICIAL OFFICERS.

ART. 163. Criminal liability may be required of judicial officers when they infringe laws relating to the exercise of their duties in the cases specifically provided for in the penal code, or in other special laws.

ART. 164. The trial of judicial liability against a judicial officer can only be instituted:

1. In virtue of a ruling of a competent court.

2. At the instance of the department of public prosecution.

3. At the instance of a person qualified to appear in court.

ART. 165. When the supreme court, on account of lawsuits or causes of which it takes cognizance, or by reason of the inspection or supervision which it exercises over its subordinates, or by any other means, is informed of any act of a judicial officer which may be classified as a crime, it shall order the institution of an action for its verification and proof, first hearing the depar:ment of public prosecution.

ART. 166. The provisions of the preceding article shall be extended to audiencias in case the act which may be classified as a crime comes within their jurisdiction.

If it should not come within their jurisdiction, they shall bring to the knowledge of the court of competent jurisdiction the facts, with the circumstances that may be useful in the proceedings.

ART. 167. Judicial officers shall limit themselves to informing the *fiscal* of the audiencia of the territory to which they belong of the facts and data they may have, in order that the latter may bring the proper criminal action, or cause it to be brought by another *fiscal* if the delinquent belongs to a different jurisdiction.

The above-mentioned officers shall also inform the presiding judge of the audiencia of the case, stating that they have already brought it to the knowledge of the *fiscal*.

ART. 168. The department of public prosecution may institute criminal proceedings:

1. In the execution of a royal order.

2. In virtue of its duty to promote the discovery and punishment of crimes.

ART. 169. The royal order which incites the department of public prosecution to institute proceedings shall specify the fact or facts that are to be cause of judicial actions.

ART. 170. When the royal order commands proceedings against a judicial officer it shall be forwarded to the *fiscal* of the audiencia of competent jurisdiction.

ART. 171. The *fiscal* of the supreme court, when he has knowledge of any fact which gives rise to demanding liability of any officer of those mentioned in the preceding article, shall issue an order to prosecute the said officer, directing this order to the *fiscal* of the proper audiencia, with the instructions he may think proper, reporting this action to the colonial department.

ART. 172. The *fiscales* of the audiencias, after receiving from the supreme court the order commanding them to institute a cause against judicial officers, shall make the complaint which may be proper according to law.

Fiscales of audiencias shall also make the corresponding denunciation without requiring a command from their hierarchical superior or the Government whenever they learn of any crime committed by a judicial officer.

ART. 173. In the cases in which *fiscales* of audiencias have knowledge that any associate justice has been guilty of an offense, they shall inform the *fiscal* of the supreme court, who shall proceed to institute the action if he deems it proper.

ART. 174. The representatives of the department of public prosecution shall make to those of the audiencias to which they are assigned the same denunciation prescribed in the preceding article relating to crimes committed by judicial officers.

ART. 175. In order that an action may be instituted with the object of exacting criminal liability of judicial officers in the third case of Article 164, a preliminary procedure must first take place in accordance with the proceedings established by the law on criminal procedure, and a declaration stating that there are grounds for prosecuting the same.

This declaration does not accept their guilt.

ART. 176. The same court which in a proper case should take cognizance of the cause, shall also take cognizance of the preliminary procedure referred to in the preceding article.

CHAPTER II.

CIVIL LIABILITY OF JUDICIAL OFFICERS.

ART. 177. The civil liability of judicial officers shall be limited to the payment of the computable loss and damage which they may cause individuals, corporations, or the State, when in the discharge of their duties they violate laws through inexcusable negligence or ignorance.

ART. 178. As computable damages for the intents and purposes of the preceding article shall be understood all damages which may be appraised in currency, according to a reasonable estimate of the courts.

ART. 179. Negligence or ignorance shall be held as inexcusable, whenever there has been made, even unintentionally, a ruling manifestly contrary to law, or whenever there has been neglected any step or formality which has been ordered to be observed under the pain of nullity.

ART. 180. Civil liability may be only exacted at the instance of the party prejudiced, or his legal representatives in an ordinary action, and before the court immediately superior to that which has incurred the same.

ART. 181. An exaction of civil liability can not be made until the sentence which has been rendered in the cause or suit which is supposed to have caused damage is final.

ART. 182. An action of civil liability can not be instituted by the person who, although he could have done so, did not make objections at the proper time during the trial.

In nò case shall a sentence pronounced in an action of civil liability alter a final sentence.

TITLE VI.

POWERS OF SUPERIOR AND INFERIOR COURTS.

CHAPTER I.

POWERS OF MUNICIPAL JUDGES AND JUSTICES OF THE PEACE.

ART. 183. Municipal judges and justices of the peace shall have power:

1. To take part in effecting acts of conciliation.

2. To exercise a voluntary jurisdiction in the cases for which they are expressly authorized by law.

3. To take cognizance in first instance and in oral trial of complaints which do not involve more than 200 pesos.

4. To dictate preliminary rulings in testamentary matters or intestate successions, whenever it is proper according to law, in towns where there is no court of first instance, until such court takes cognizance of the same.

By preliminary rulings for the purposes of this article shall be understood those the object of which is to place in securi'y the property of inheritances and to provide for everything which admits of no delay.

Whenever municipal judges or justices of the peace take part in these proceedings they shall immediately report the fact to the court of first instance, to which they shall forward copies of the proceedings they may have instituted.

5. To make, in cases requiring a decision which can not be delayed without causing damage to the interested parties, provisional rulings, reporting the matter to the court of first instance and sending the data at the same time.

6. To carry out the auxiliary commissions which are intrusted to them by judges of first instance or by audiencias.

7. To take cognizance of the other actions that are intrusted to them by law.

ART. 184. In penal matters municipal judges or justices of the peace shall have the power:

1: To take cognizance of offenses in first instance.

2. To take a preventive preliminary action in criminal causes.

3. To carry out the auxiliary commissions intrusted to them by examining judges, judges of first instance, or by audiencias.

CHAPTER II.

POWERS OF EXAMINING AND FIRST INSTANCE JUDGES.

ART. 185. Examining and first instance judges shall have the power:

In civil matters, to discharge the duties which are expressly assigned to them by law and the commissions with which they are intrusted by audiencias for carrying on certain proceedings.

In criminal matters, to make the preliminary examinations in the causes and to institute the other proceedings referred to them by audiencias.

In civil and criminal matters, to discharge the auxiliary commissions addressed to them by other judges or courts through the proper audiencia.

CHAPTER III.

POWERS OF AUDIENCIAS.

ART. 186. The civil chambers of audiencias shall have the power:

1. To decide questions of competency raised in civil matters between municipal judges or justices of the peace of their districts belonging to different subdistricts.

2. To decide questions of competency in civil matters between judges of first instance of their district.

3. To take cognizance of recourses of coercion in civil matters raised against ecclesiastical judges, either subordinate or chief (subroganeos ó metropolitanos).

4. To take cognizance on appeal for review only (única instancia) of interlocutory issues (incidentes) in civil matters when they relate to challenges of their associate justices.

5. To take cognizance in first instance of actions exacting civil liability instituted against municipal judges, or justices of the peace, and judges of first instance.

6. To take cognizance in second instance—

Of civil causes and matters which were in first instance taken cognizance of by judges of first instance of their territory.

Of interlocutory issues in challenges of judges of first instance.

7. To aid in the administration of justice in civil matters whenever such aid is demanded of them by other judges or courts.

ART. 187. Besides the incidental issues, the cognizance of which the law on criminal procedure assigns to the competency of criminal chambers and audiencias and to territorial audiencias, they shall also take cognizance:

Criminal chambers and audiencias, of all the causes for crimes committed within their respective province or limits and belonging to the ordinary jurisdiction, with the exception of those which are at the time being taken cognizance of by the supreme court, and with the other exceptions prescribed in this decree-law or in special laws.

Criminal chambers of territorial audiencias of causes referring to crimes committed in the exercise of their functions, within their respective territory:

1. By provincial deputies.

2. By members of municipal councils in the capitals of provinces and towns where there is an audiencia.

3. By administrative authorities of the said towns, with the exception of the civil and military governors.

Territorial audiencias *in banc* shall take cognizance of causes in all classes of crimes committed by auxiliary officers of the department of public prosecution of the criminal audiencias.

TITLE VII.

AUXILIARY OFFICERS OF SUPERIOR AND INFERIOR COURTS.

ART. 188. Under the denomination of auxiliary officers of superior and inferior courts there shall be understood:

Judicial secretaries.

Judicial archivists.

Officers of chambers.

Recording clerks (*escribanos de actuaciones*).

Clerks attending as witnesses (*actuarios testigos de asistencia*).

CHAPTER I.

JUDICIAL SECRETARIES.

ART. 189. There shall be secretaries:

Of municipal courts or courts of justices of the peace.

Of examining courts.

Of chambers of justice of the territorial audiencias.

Of administration of the territorial audiencias.

There shall also be secretaries and vice-secretaries of the criminal audiencias.

SECTION 1.—*Conditions common to judicial secretaries.*

ART. 190. In order to be a secretary of whatsoever class or denomination it shall be necessary:

1. To possess the qualifications required by article 73 of this decree law for the offices of judges and associate justices.

2. Not to be included in any of the cases of incapacity specified for the same in article 50.

3. Not to accept any of the offices or employments which are incompatible with judicial functions according to article 75.

From this provision are excepted the secretaries of municipal judges or justices of the peace, in the cases specified in this decree-law.

ART. 191. Persons who have anything to do with proposing and appointing judicial secretaries shall take care to ascertain whether the candidates possess the qualifications required by this decree-law, or whether for any cause whatsoever they are incapacitated to accept the position to be filled.

ART. 192. In cases of offices to be filled by competitive examinations the provisions of the foregoing article must be fulfilled before the examinations begin, only those persons being admitted to the same who are not legally disqualified.

Those who have obtained incompatible employments or offices shall be admitted to the examinations, if they declare that in case they obtain the position they seek they will renounce the one which is incompatible with the same.

ART. 193. Holding offices of secretaries of inferior or superior courts shall be a justifiable cause for being exempted from the obligatory offices mentioned in No. 3, of article 190, the express provisions of articles 76 and 77 of this decree law with respect to judges and associate justices being also applicable to judicial secretaries.

ART. 194. Judicial secretaries, before taking possession of their offices, shall take an oath to observe the constitution of the State, to be faithful to the King, and to diligently comply with the laws referring to the exercise of their office.

This oath shall be taken:

By the secretaries of municipal courts or of courts of justices of the peace and examining courts, before the judge whom they are to assist.

By the secretaries of chambers of justice of territorial audiencias, and by the secretaries and vice-secretaries of criminal audiencias, before the chamber of audiencia in which they are to discharge their duties.

By the secretaries of administration of territorial audiencias, before the chamber of administration of the respective audiencia.

ART. 195. The respective judges or chambers shall install the secretaries into their offices immediately after they have been sworn in.

ART. 196. It shall be the duty of the secretaries of municipal or courts of justices of the peace, examining courts, and chambers of justice of audiencias, as well as of recording clerks (*escribanos de actuaciones*), and of clerks attending as witnesses (*actuarios testigos de asistencia*):

1. To aid judges, chambers, and courts, according to their respective duties, in all that refers to the exercise of voluntary or litigated jurisdiction in civil and criminal matters.

2. To keep secret all matters and cases they may have charge of which require it.

3. To make notes in documents of the days and hours in cases in which the terms are fatal (fatales), when the papers are presented to them, giving a receipt therefor.

4. To make notes, in a similar manner, of the days on which parties

take and return documents, and dates on which they present papers without returning the same.

5. To give a timely account of all the claims which are presented to them in matters in which they take part during the day's session, or at least that of the preceding day, being responsible for unjustifiable delays incurred by them.

6. To draw up correctly and to certify with their names proceedings, rulings, documents, and sentences which pass through their hands.

7. To keep in their custody and to preserve with the greatest care the proceedings of trials and the documents that are in their charge.

8. Not to give any certified copies or certificates except by virtue of a ruling of the superior or inferior court.

9. To always keep up to date the books provided for in the regulations.

10. To be impartial to all who have business pending in their offices.

11. To fulfill all the other obligations imposed upon them by law and by the provisions of the regulations.

ART. 197. Secretaries of examining courts and those of chambers of justice of audiencias, as well as recording clerks (*escribanos de actuaciones*), besides the obligations prescribed in the preceding article, shall have the following:

1. To give oral accounts when rulings on procedure are in question which do not require complicated precedents for their solution.

2. To give a written account, with the greatest precision possible, when rulings on procedure are in question which require written accounts by reason of their importance, the volume of precedents, or the difficulties which they present for their solution.

3. To draw up the judicial reports for the consideration of the actions and causes, when considered both for interlocutory and for definitive decisions.

4. To show in the judicial reports whether the documents are in good state for deciding the article, action, or cause, or whether there is some serious defect which must be corrected, as its omission might be a cause for nullity.

5. To show, in cases of appeals, whether the decisions of first instance, and, in cases of cassation, whether those of second instance were pronounced within the period provided for by law.

6. To put on the margin of rulings the surnames of the judges and associate justices who may have attended and the names and surnames of the same on the margins of documents and decisions.

7. To incorporate in the minutes of considerations the days of their duration, the number of hours employed each day, and the names and surnames of the defendants who attended them.

8. To see that there is no ruling left without being rubricated by the presiding judge of chamber, nor any document or decision without that of those who take part in making them.

9. To draw up and countersign royal writs, letters, or dispatches after they have been signed by the presiding judge of the court and the associate justices whose duty it is to do so.

10. To regulate costs according to the schedule of fees and bills of lawyers in cases in which a party has been required to pay them.

11. To fulfill the other obligations imposed upon them by laws and the provisions of the regulations.

ART. 198. Judicial secretaries shall reside in the town in which they perform their duties. They can not absent themselves without leave granted them by the judge or the presiding judge of the respective court.

Those who absent themselves without leave shall suffer a disciplinary correction; and if they are absent for three months or more, or if they do not appear upon being summoned, they shall lose their office.

ART. 199. The regulations shall specify:

1. The days and hours on which offices of secretaries and clerks shall be open, which shall appear on a placard posted on the outside of their offices.

2. The number of books that shall be kept by secretaries and clerks, and conditions regulating them.

3. The manner and time fixed for making inventories of the books and papers.

4. The method of distribution of business among secretaries and clerks of the same inferior or superior court.

ART. 200. Judicial secretaries shall be transferred, suspended, or discharged from their career, or retired, for any of the causes specified in Title IV of this decree-law.

ART. 201. When, because of extraordinary or unforeseen circumstances, the number of secretaries necessary for the administration of justice and for the transaction of administration business is lacking, the judge or the presiding judge of the court shall appoint one or more if they are necessary, giving immediately to the Government an account of the causes which rendered said appointment indispensable, which shall be only of a temporary character.

ART. 202. Secretaries of courts of examination in considering actions and causes and in all solemn acts shall wear black clothes.

Secretaries of audiencias shall always use a lawyer's gown without any other distinctive mark.

SECTION 2.—*Secretaries of municipal courts or of courts of justices of the peace.*

ART. 203. In each municipal court there shall be a secretary, who shall certify all its acts, and a substitute for cases of vacancy, sickness, absence, incompatibility, challenge, or any other impediment of the secretary.

ART. 204. For employment as secretaries of municipal courts or courts of justices of the peace, preference shall be given to those who have some legal knowledge acquired in professional studies or in the transaction of judicial business.

ART. 205. The secretaries of municipal courts or of courts of justices of the peace, and their substitutes, shall be appointed by judges of first instance from among three persons proposed by the municipal judges.

Their emoluments shall consist of the fees fixed by the schedules of judicial fees.

ART. 206. The office of judicial secretary, and of his substitute, of municipal courts shall be compatible with any public employments or offices the duties of which may be conciliated with it in towns, the population of which does not reach 500 inhabitants.

In those where the population exceeds this number such offices shall be incompatible with any employment, office, or commission paid by the Government, by the province, or by the towns.

SECTION 3.—Secretaries of courts of examination.

ART. 207. There shall be eight positions of judicial secretaries for criminal affairs in Habana, and two in San Juan de Puerto Rico, two secretaries being assigned to each court of examination.

These officers shall have the rank and draw the salary of judges of first instance of the entrance category.

The costs which, were they not salaried, they would receive according to the schedule of fees, shall be turned into the public treasury, on the proper paper for payments to the State, as fast as they are collected.

ART. 208. Secretaries of courts of examination shall replace each other in cases of vacancies, sickness, absence, incompatibility, challenges, or any other legitimate impediment.

ART. 209. The clerks employed in courts of first instance shall discharge the duties of secretaries of examination, and vacancies shall continue to be filled according to the regulations in force.

SECTION 4.—Secretaries of territorial audiencias.

ART. 210. There shall be in each audiencia one secretary of administration acting as secretary of the court <i>in banc</i>, of the chamber of administration, and of the presiding judge's office.

ART. 211. Secretaries of administration shall be engaged exclusively in the administrative matters of audiencias, without taking part directly or indirectly in matters of a litigative character, except in directing them in a proper way in their relations with the presiding judge's office.

ART. 212. Secretaries of administration shall furthermore be obliged:

1. To preserve the seal of the court.

2. To seal and register royal writs, letters, and dispatches which the court orders to be issued to the parties concerned or officially.

3. To keep an exact register in which the documents mentioned in the preceding article shall be copied literally, and not to give any copy

of said documents without a written order from the court or from one of its chambers.

4. To take charge of the archives of the court in the character and capacity of keeper of archives, with the powers and liabilities of that office in courts where there is no special keeper of archives.

5. To take charge of the library in the courts in which there is no keeper of archives.

ART. 213. The Government may create the office of vice-secretary of administration in any audiencia whenever the accumulation of business renders such course necessary or advisable.

ART. 214. It shall be 'the duty of vice-secretaries to replace secretaries in cases of vacancies, absence, sickness, or any legal impediment occurring in particular cases, and to assist them in all that refers to the discharge of their duties, in accordance with the distribution of the business of the secretary's office.

ART. 215. Vice-secretaries, officials of the secretary's office, and clerks paid out of the budget, and those of either class who are paid from the appropriation for material, shall be under the direct orders of the secretaries and presiding judges.

ART. 216. The officers and clerks of a secretary's office, paid out of the budget, shall be subject in their appointment and qualifications to the general rules fixed for public employees under the same conditions.

Those who draw their pay from the appropriation for material, as assigned to them by the internal regulations of the secretary's office, may be freely appointed, suspended, or discharged by the presiding judge of the respective court.

SECTION 5.—*Secretaries and vice-secretaries of criminal audiencias.*

ART. 217. In each criminal audiencia there shall be a secretary and a vice-secretary, whenever the needs of the service require it.

ART. 218. The vice-secretaries shall perform the duties of the secretaries when they are assigned to a particular chamber or section, and when they do not attend the latter, besides substituting them in cases of vacancies or impediments.

The fees fixed in the schedules for secretaries and vice-secretaries shall be collected in paper and turned into the treasury.

ART. 219. The presiding judges of courts shall appoint lawyers as substitute secretaries to replace regular secretaries in cases of vacancies or impediments.

Lawyers acting as substitutes shall have the same privileges as are granted to substitutes of the department of public prosecution.

In case of urgent necessity, courts in substituting secretaries may avail themselves of the services of officers of chamber who are lawyers, or who are qualified to perform the duties of notaries, or of the services of any secretary of an inferior court.

CHAPTER II.

ARCHIVISTS.

ART. 220. In such audiencias in which the office of keeper of archives is considered by the Government to be necessary or convenient on account of the importance and extension of their archives, there shall be an archivist with the subordinate employees necessary for the custody, preservation, and classification of documents.

ART. 221. Archivists shall be proposed in ternary by the chamber of administration of the respective audiencia, and shall be appointed by the colonial department.

ART. 222. Court archivists shall have notarial authority in certificates which they may issue relating to records on file in their archives. They can not issue them except by virtue of a judicial ruling or by order of the presiding judge of the court.

· ART. 223. In courts which have a library it shall be under the care of the archivists.

ART. 224. The employees of judicial archives of courts shall be under the direct orders of the archivists and the latter under those of the presiding judge of the court.

ART. 225. The archivists and the employees of archives shall have a fixed salary. The fees for the certifications they may issue shall be collected in paper and turned into the treasury.

CHAPTER III.

OFFICERS OF CHAMBER.

ART. 226. In every audiencia there shall be officers of chamber.

ART. 227. It shall be the duty of officers of chamber to issue summons, citations, and notifications, attachments, collection of decrees, and other duties which should not take place in the presence of the court, and which are peculiar to the court to which said officers belong.

To assist the presiding judge of the court and the presiding judges of chambers, under whose orders they are, to carry out those relating to the judicial service which may be given them.

To attend court rooms whenever the presiding judge of the chamber to which they belong orders them to attend on account of special circumstances, taking care that persons attending the court preserve order and decorum.

ART. 228. Officers of chamber shall be appointed by the Government on the recommendation of the respective courts.

ART. 229. In order to become an officer of chamber, a candidate must be a lawyer, or have completed and qualified himself in studies required for offices of public certification, or possess a knowledge of judicial practice relating to the office he is to fill. The latter qualification shall be proven by examination before a board composed of three secretaries of chamber appointed by the presiding judge of the respective court.

If there should not be this number, it shall be completed by attorneys practicing in the locality.

ART. 230. Officers of chamber shall be sworn in at a public session before the proper court.

ART. 231. The formula of the oath of office taken by officers of chamber shall consist of the pledges to be faithful to the King, to observe the constitution and laws, and to satisfactorily perform the duties of their offices.

ART. 232. Officers of chamber shall be paid the salaries provided for them in the budget. The fees that are assigned them in the schedule of fees shall be collected in paper and turned into the treasury.

ART. 233. Officers of chamber shall not leave the capital except in cases when chambers of audiencia or extraordinary chambers are convened outside thereof, and always by a special ruling of the presiding judge of the audiencia.

ART. 234. Suspension and discharge of officers of chamber and secretaries of municipal or courts of justices of the peace may be decided upon by the presiding judge of the audiencia or the judge of first instance of the subdistrict, respectively, subject to the provisions of Chapters II and III of Title IV of this decree-law.

Presiding judges of audiencias shall report to the colonial department of the use they may have made of this power, in order to arrive at the final decision which may be proper.

CHAPTER IV.

Section 1.—*Recording clerks (escribanos de actuaciones) of Cuba and Puerto Rico.*

ART. 235. Every court of first instance of the final category of the island of Cuba shall have at least six recording clerkships (*escribanías de actuaciones*), three of the promotion and two of the entrance category, without prejudice to increasing said number after proceedings, in which the necessity of new appointments is demonstrated by a judge or by the respective chamber of administration.

In Puerto Rico the number of clerkships in each court of first instance of the final category shall be three, and in those of the promotion or entrance category there shall be two at least.

ART. 236. The present clerkships shall be retained, although they exceed the number fixed in the foregoing provisions; but vacancies hereafter occurring shall not be filled until the prescribed number remains.

Matters of legal procedure pending in a clerk's office or offices that shall hereafter become vacant shall be turned over, after an inventory is made, to the general distribution of civil affairs, the archives remaining in the office of the secretary of administration of the inferior court to which they belong.

ART. 237. In towns having several inferior courts, whenever any of the same has a number of clerks exceeding by more than one the number existing in the other inferior courts of the same place, the chamber of administration of the audiencia shall transfer the clerk last appointed from the court with the greatest number of clerks, to the court with the smallest number. The transferred clerk shall continue to perform his duties relating to the matters which have been apportioned to him before the transfer and which are in course of procedure.

The presiding judge of the audiencia shall make a report of these transfers to the general direction of grace and justice of the colonial department.

ART. 238. The recording clerks' offices of courts of first instance of said islands shall be filled by competition on the recommendation in ternary made by the chambers of administration of the proper territorial audiencias.

ART. 239. When a vacancy occurs in an office of recording clerk the proper judge of the subdistrict shall state to the chamber of administration of the audiencia of the territory whether he considers filling the vacancy in question as necessary or not.

In the former case, when the vacancy exceeds the number fixed in article 1, he shall state to the chamber of administration the grounds on which his opinion is based, reporting the number of clerks on duty at the court and attaching a statement of the judicial business, civil, criminal, as well as administrative, of which he took cognizance during the last two years. In view of this data the chamber of administration shall submit the proceedings with its report to the colonial department in order that the latter may decide whether the vacancy should be filled or not.

ART. 240. When it is thought necessary to fill an office of recording clerk the decision shall be communicated to the presiding judge of the proper audiencia in order that the latter may advertise the competition in the official newspapers of the island to which belongs the court in which the vacancy exists, to enable those desiring to obtain the position to present within the period of thirty days, counting from the publication of the advertisement, their petitions in writing to the judge of first instance of the subdistrict.

ART. 241. If the vacancy does not exceed the number fixed in article 235 for each inferior court, the presiding judge of the audiencia shall publish at once an advertisement for the competition in the same manner as determined in the foregoing article.

ART. 242. In order to be a recording clerk the following qualifications are required:

1. To be a Spaniard and a layman.
2. To be over twenty-five years of age.
3. To be of good moral character.
4. To be a lawyer or to have passed the course required for the notarial career and to have obtained the proper certificate of fitness to

issue certifications for a notarial office, or to have served temporarily as recording clerk for the period of two years.

ART. 243. Those who do not possess the qualifications mentioned in No. 4 of the foregoing article may also aspire to the office of a recording clerk, but candidates of this class shall be appointed only when candidates possessing the same are wanting, and shall fill the office only until the time when the position is sought for by a person who possesses said qualifications, or until the vacancy is announced again, if such course is thought to be advisable.

ART. 244. The following persons can not be appointed recording clerks:

1. Bankrupts or insolvents who have not secured their discharge.

2. Debtors to the State or to public funds, as taxpayers, or for balance of account.

3. Persons under criminal prosecution during the period thereof. .

4. Persons sentenced to corporeal punishment until they obtain rehabilitation.

ART. 245. The office of recording clerk shall be incompatible with the office of a deputy to the Cortes, provincial deputy, municipal judge or justice of the peace, or assessor of the same when acting as judge of first instance, alcalde or member of a municipal council, practicing law and with any office or employment which confers additional jurisdiction or is paid from the funds of the State, province, or municipality, or which obliges them to live away from their domicile.

ART. 246. When the period referred to in articles 239 and 240 has elapsed, judges of first instance shall forward to the presiding judge of the proper territorial audiencia the petitions and documents presented by the candidates, making a report on each one of the same.

ART. 247. The chamber of administration, in view of the petitions and documents received, and after procuring the data it may consider necessary with regard to the morality, conduct, and diligence of the candidates, and taking also into account the services which they may have rendered in the administration of justice, shall submit to the colonial department a recommendation in ternary for the position to be filled, accompanying therewith the personal records of the persons proposed and an extract of the records of the other candidates.

ART. 248. In making the recommendation the chambers of administration shall give preference in the first place to those who are lawyers, and, if these are wanting, to those who have passed and qualified themselves in courses for the offices of notaries and who have the proper diploma. From among several candidates who served as recording clerks the preference shall be given to the one who performed the duties of a clerk for the longest time in an inferior court of the highest category.

ART. 249. The appointment of recording clerks shall be made by the colonial department and must be given to one of the persons recommended.

ART. 250. The clerk elect shall take possession of his office within the period of sixty days without prejudice to reducing said period if the convenience of the service demands such action, or to grant to appointees the extensions they may ask, which may be conceded if the convenience of the service permits of it, the presentation of the credentials given the appointee being sufficient for taking possession of office after the orders of appointment have been communicated. The appointee who does not present himself to take possession within the designated period, shall be considered as renouncing the office unless he gives adequate written proofs of his impossibility to do so, in which case he shall be granted the extension which may be considered sufficient.

ART. 251. If an appointment becomes null on account of the failure of the appointee to appear to take possession of the office, the colonial department shall make another appointment from among the candidates included in the ternary, without the necessity of new proceedings.

ART. 252. Recording clerks elect, before taking possession of their offices, shall take before the proper judges an oath of allegiance to the king and to fulfill all the obligations imposed on them by law.

The oath of office having once been taken, a new oath for the office of recording clerk shall not be required.

An appointee shall be given a certificate viséd by the judge, stating that he has been sworn in and has taken possession of office, and the judge shall communicate this fact to the presiding judge of the audiencia, who shall report the same to the general direction of grace and justice of the colonial department.

Discharges shall be effected in the same manner, the cause being specified.

ART. 253. Recording clerks shall substitute each other in cases of vacancies, sickness, absence, incompatibility, challenge, or other legitimate impediment. In every court there shall be kept a list of successors for these substitutions.

ART. 254. Recording clerks shall not draw any other pay than that which corresponds to them according to the schedules of judicial fees.

ART. 255. Recording clerks may be discharged in the following cases after proceedings, and after hearing the parties concerned:

1. When they are included in any of the cases of incapacity established in article 243, or any incompatibility of those specified in article 244.

2. When they have undergone a disciplinary punishment for serious acts, which, without being crimes, compromise the dignity of their office or lower them in the public esteem.

3. When they are declared civilly liable.

4. When, on account of their vicious conduct, their dishonorable bearing, or habitual negligence, they do not deserve to continue to fill their offices.

ART. 256. The presiding judge of the proper audiencia, if he thinks it proper, and in view of the reports and data he obtains concerning the correctness of the alleged facts, may grant recording clerks a leave of four months. If the leave is solicited in order to leave the island, or for a greater period, it may be granted only by the colonial department, or advanced by the Governor-General in case of urgency and with the requisites prescribed for leaves of officers of the administration of justice.

The Governor-General and the presiding judge of an audiencia, in a proper case, shall report to the colonial department or to the general direction of grace and justice of the same, the leaves which they advance or grant, specifying the reasons for the same, as well as of the leaves which they refuse; also stating the causes for their refusal.

ART. 257. Notaries who are at the same time recording clerks, as they fill one of the alienated public certification offices, shall continue in the same under the rules established in this decree, preserving the power to renounce the judicial office in favor of the State.

ART. 258. Recording clerks who are at the present time filling these offices in the character of temporary officers, shall also continue to perform them in the same character, being strictly subject to the provisions of this decree-law.

ART. 259. In the procedure of filling offices of recording clerks which may be in progress in inferior courts or in audiencias at the time of the publication of this decree-law, the provisions of the same shall be observed, and said proceedings shall be submitted at the proper time to the colonial department with the proper recommendation in ternary.

ART. 260. Recording clerks shall use as a distinctive mark in the acts of their profession a silver medal smaller than that used by judges, suspended from a black string with a black pin with a silver thread, showing on the obverse the attributes of Justice and on the reverse the inscription, "Fe pública judicial."

ART. 261. Recording clerks shall have the power to recommend to the chamber of administration of the proper territorial audiencia through the same inferior court in which they serve, and after demonstrating to the said court the necessity of the appointment, a person to assist them in performing their duties, and who must possess all the qualifications required by this decree-law for the performance of said duties by the incumbent.

Said auxiliary officers shall be appointed by the chamber of administration, if their ability is considered sufficient and the appointment is necessary to assist the recording clerk, under the guaranty and liability of the latter, the remuneration for this service being charged to the recording clerk, who shall have the power to discharge his assistants freely and recommend others both in case of discharge or resignation as well as in case of death.

The presiding judges of territorial audiencias shall report to the general direction of grace and justice of the colonial department the appointments and discharges of assistants to recording clerks.

ART. 262. Notaries who at the present time discharge both duties in the capacity of regular incumbents filling offices alienated by means of the proper diploma shall continue filling the office of recording clerks in the places assigned for their offices by their respective diplomas, as long as the vacancies are not effected in a natural or legal way, or as long as their resignation from the judicial office is not accepted.

ART. 263. Notaries appointed in accordance with the law of February 15, 1889, or the decree of September 16, 1874, may be authorized by audiencias, reporting on the matter to the government according to temporary provison number 5 of that law, to serve in commission and provisionally as recording clerks of courts of first instance where their notarial office is situated and wherever necessity demands it.

ART. 264. Notaries, who in accordance with the provisions of the foregoing article have obtained said authorization, shall be relieved from said clerks' offices whenever in the judgment of the chambers of administration of the respective audiencias they can be replaced by persons who have completed the course for the notarial profession at the University of Manila, or at any other university of the Kingdom, and possess the first three conditions of article 242.

If there be no such persons, they may be replaced by those possessing the qualification stated in number 4 of the said article, and if there should also be none such, by the persons possessing those of article 243.

ART. 265. These appointments shall be made by the presiding judge of the respective audiencias and shall be called temporary clerks, and taking into consideration the needs of each inferior court and after fixing the number of clerks for each one of them, he shall make a report to the colonial department.

ART. 266. Where there are no regular incumbents of alienated offices or notaries public, and neither is it possible to make the temporary appointments referred to in the foregoing article, they shall be replaced in the exercise of the judicial office by those attending as witnesses in conformity with the laws and provisions in force at the present time.

ART. 267. Concerning the organization and administration of recording clerks, offices, the personnel of the Philippines shall be subject to the provisions of the corresponding articles of the foregoing section.

CHAPTER V.

CLERKS ATTENDING AS WITNESSES.

ART. 268. In the Philippine Islands justices of the peace and petty governors (gobernadorcillos), in a proper case, shall perform their duties in the presence of one attending witness, who must be of age, in the enjoyment of his civil rights, and be able to read and write Spanish.

ART. 269. Attending witnesses shall perform the duties of recording clerks of courts of justices of the peace, subject to the prescriptions of the law on civil procedure, and shall be appointed by the said judges and petty governors, who may appoint a different person for each affair of which they take cognizance.

ART. 270. Clerks attending as witnesses shall receive the fees fixed in the schedule of judicial fees, which is now or may hereafter be in force.

TITLE VIII.

SUBORDINATE OFFICERS OF INFERIOR AND SUPERIOR COURTS.

FIRST AND LAST CHAPTER.

ART. 271. Under the name of subordinate officers of superior and inferior courts there shall be understood janitors, constables, messengers, and office attendants.

ART. 272. In each municipal court or court of justices of the peace there shall be at least one subordinate officer called a constable (alguacil); he shall discharge the various duties which are to be performed by subordinate officers according to the provisions of this decree-law.

ART. 273. In municipal courts or courts of justices of the peace in which more than one subordinate officer is required, the judge shall recommend to the proper judge of first instance the number and class of those that should be appointed; and the latter shall send the recommendation with his report to the presiding judge of the audiencia, who shall decide what he may consider proper.

ART. 274. The Government shall designate the number and class of subordinate officers to be employed:

By courts of examination and of first instance in view of the recommendation made by the judges and the reports of the chambers of administration of audiencias.

By audiencias, in view of the information given by the respective chambers of administration.

ART. 275. To be a subordinate officer of an inferior or a superior court, it is necessary to be a Spaniard, over twenty-five years of age; to know how to read and write; to observe good conduct, and not to have suffered any corporeal or correctional punishments.

A third part of the subordinate offices of each class in courts of examination and first instance, in audiencias, shall be filled by persons discharged from the army or navy, with a good record in the service.

ART. 276. Examining judges, judges of first instance, and presiding judges of superior courts shall appoint the subordinate officers of their respective superior and inferior courts.

ART. 277. Whenever a person is appointed as a subordinate officer who does not possess the qualifications specified in article 275, his appointment shall be declared void by the officer who may have made the same.

ART. 278. If the officer who appointed a subordinate officer without the necessary qualifications does not declare the appointment void, it shall be so decreed:

By the judge of first instance, in the case of subordinate officers of municipal courts.

By presiding judges of audiencias, in the case of subordinate officers of examining and first-instance courts.

By the presiding judge of the supreme court, in the cases of subordinate officers of audiencias.

ART. 279. The janitors and constables shall fulfill all the obligations imposed upon them by the laws and regulations; they shall obey the orders they may receive from judges and presiding judges of the courts and chambers to which they belong; they shall guard the chamber, assist secretaries of administration and of justice, and officers of chamber in the transaction of the judicial business, and in the duties which they must perform in carrying out the orders of superior courts, and they can not excuse themselves from obeying them, without prejudice to their making complaint to their respective hierarchical superiors of any offenses against them.

ART. 280. The messengers and office attendants shall have charge of the mechanical work designated by the internal regulations of inferior and superior courts, and shall carry out the orders of their superiors.

Judges and presiding judges of superior courts may appoint them to perform the duties of janitors and constables.

ART. 281. The subordinate officers of audiencias shall leave the capital only by express orders of the presiding judge, in the cases when chambers of audiencia convene away from the same.

ART. 282. Judges and presiding judges of superior courts shall establish the regulations for the service of subordinate officers in the manner they may consider most advisable.

ART. 283. The subordinate officers of inferior and superior courts may be suspended and discharged freely by the officers who have the power of appointing them.

There shall be no appeal from the decision of these officers.

ART. 284. The subordinate officers of municipal courts shall not receive any other remuneration than that fixed in the schedules of judicial fees.

ART. 285. The Government, after hearing the examining or first-instance judges, and the chambers of administration of audiencias, shall fix the amount which may be necessary to pay or complete the salaries of the subordinate officers of inferior and superior courts, when the remuneration assigned to them by law in the schedules of judicial fees is not sufficient.

ART. 286. Subordinate officers shall replace each other in case the number of these officers is insufficient for a good service, the provisions prescribed in this decree-law for judicial secretaries being observed.

ART. 287. Subordinate officers of audiencias, while in service within the court or when they assist with the latter in public business, shall wear the uniform prescribed for them.

TITLE IX.

GOVERNMENT AND ADMINISTRATION OF SUPERIOR COURTS.

CHAPTER I.

PRESIDING JUDGES OF TERRITORIAL AUDIENCIAS.

ART. 288. The government of audiencias shall be in charge of their presiding judges.

ART. 289. Presiding judges of audiencias, besides the powers and obligations which are ascribed to them in other articles of this decree law, shall have the following ones:

1. To observe and cause to be observed this decree-law and all other provisions which refer, respectively, to the duties they discharge.

2. To cause due order to be observed in courts by associate justices, auxiliary and subordinate officers.

3. To recommend to the Government whatever they may consider necessary or advisable, in order to make the administration of justice more complete.

4. To receive and send out the official correspondence.

5. To pass, with their reports, petitions, complaints, and consultations which the superior court *in banc*, the chambers, and the associate justices of the court, its auxiliary or subordinate officers, submit to the colonial department, in conformity with the provisions of this decree-law.

6. To convene and preside over the court *in banc* and over the chamber of administration.

7. To receive excuses for nonattendance of associate justices, auxiliary and subordinate officers, and to report said excuses to the proper presiding judge of the chamber.

8. To name the associate justices necessary to make up the requisite number for a given matter whenever the members of one chamber are not sufficient with those of another chamber, observing the greatest equality in this service.

9. To order on all working days, at the hour assigned for holding sessions, that the court resolve itself into chambers of justice.

10. To preside, whenever they deem it proper, over any chamber of justice without prejudice to doing so in the cases expressly ordered by law. In the court rooms, while presiding, they have the right to speak, while no other person can do so without their permission.

11. To take care that all the associate justices, auxiliary and subordinate officers strictly carry out their duties to communicate to them the orders which they may deem proper relative to the performance of their duties, and to privately admonish those who show little diligence in complying therewith.

12. To call the *fiscal* to make such observations as they deem proper for the better administration of justice, relating to him and to his subordinates, without communicating directly with the latter, or restricting the liberty of action which is due the department of public prosecution.

Whenever they consider such action necessary, they may direct themselves to the Government, making such remarks relating to the department of public prosecution as they think proper.

13. To bring to the knowledge of the proper authorities offenses of associate justices which give rise to disciplinary punishments, and to the knowledge of the competent court the crimes they may commit in the exercise of their duties.

14. To report to the Government the vacancies that occur, the entering and leaving the office by associate justices, judges, and auxiliary officers of the territory of the court, when they are appointed, promoted, transferred, retired, or discharged, or while on leave of absence.

15. To hear complaints referring to the administration of justice, brought before them by the parties concerned in causes or lawsuits on account of delay of business; to adopt the measures lying within their power, and to report the same to the respective chamber whenever the importance of the matter requires such action.

16. To appoint, besides the subordinate officers whom they have a right to appoint according to this decree-law, the employees of the secretary's office whose salaries are paid from the appropriation for material; to give them leaves of absence, and to discharge them at will.

17. To adopt the measures that are necessary or advisable to keep in good order and preservation the archives and libraries of superior courts.

18. To notify the persons who are to replace them whenever they themselves can not attend.

ART. 290. Presiding judges of audiencias shall, besides, have the power to demand, personally, directly of the judges of first instance and examination and the municipal judges of their district, the lawsuits, causes, or proceedings that have been finished or carried to full execution, whenever the matter concerns the administration of justice or the State, returning them to the superior or inferior court from which said proceedings were taken as soon as the examination which was the cause of their demand has been made.

They may also order, after consulting the board of administration, visits of inspection for the purpose of examining the state of the administration of justice in any particular superior or inferior court, whenever there are good grounds for doing so, after hearing the administrative board.

ART. 291. After presiding judges have ordered superior courts to resolve themselves into chambers of justice, they shall dispatch the correspondence and other business of their office, authorizing with their signatures the communications that should not be directed with the signature of the secretary only.

ART. 292. When the transaction of the affairs mentioned in the foregoing article has been completed, the presiding judge shall give a hearing to the interested parties who desire to make a complaint, proceeding, as is proper, in accordance with No. 15 of article 289.

ART. 293. No judge, associate justice, chamber, or superior court can submit directly to the colonial department requests referring to their office or to the affairs of the court to which they belong, except through the hierarchical superiors specified below:

Municipal judges or justices of the peace, examining or first instance judges, through the presiding judges of the respective territorial audiencias.

Associate justices of audiencias and their chambers, and audiencias *in banc* through the presiding judges of the same.

Presiding judges, in passing on the requests in question, shall state whatever they deem expedient concerning the same.

ART. 294. From the provisions of the preceding article there shall be excepted the statements directed to the Government in complaint against any of the hierarchical superiors mentioned in the said article, in which case this requirement and all that refers thereto shall be omitted.

ART. 295. In cases of vacancies of the office of the presiding judge of an audiencia, and in cases of sickness, absence, or any other just impediment, the duties of this office shall be performed by the presiding judge of chamber of greatest seniority, without prejudice to the latter continuing to preside over his own chamber whenever the duties of presiding in the court permit it.

CHAPTER II.

PRESIDING JUDGES OF CHAMBERS OF AUDIENCIAS.

ART. 296. Presiding judges of chamber shall have the obligation to observe and cause to be observed the laws referring to the office they fill; to preside over chambers to which they belong; to have the right of speech, no other person being allowed to have it without their permission; to take care that due order is preserved in their chambers, and to bring to the knowledge of the presiding judge whatever they deem advisable for making the administration of justice more effective, and the offenses of the associate justices when they think that said offenses call for a punishment not included within the limit of their powers.

ART. 297. In cases of vacancies, absence, sickness, or any other legitimate impediment of a presiding judge of a chamber, he shall be replaced by the associate justice of greatest seniority of the same.

CHAPTER III.

ADMINISTRATION AND GOVERNMENT OF CRIMINAL AUDIENCIAS AND CRIMINAL CHAMBERS OF TERRITORIAL AUDIENCIAS.

ART. 298. For the administration and government of criminal audiencias their presiding judges shall have the following duties:

1. To observe and cause to be observed this decree-law and all the laws referring to officers who are compelled to do so by reason of their office.

2. To cause proper order to be observed in courts by associate justices, auxiliary and subordinate officers.

3. To receive and dispatch official correspondence.

4. To take care that all the associate justices and auxiliary and subordinate officers comply with their duties strictly; to communicate to them the orders which they may deem advisable relating to the performance of the same, and to admonish privately those officers who show little diligence in the performance of their duties.

5. To bring to the knowledge of the proper authorities the offenses of associate justices which give rise to disciplinary punishment, and to the proper courts the crimes committed by said officers while performing their duties.

6. To report to the Government any vacancies that occur on entering and leaving the office by associate justices, judges, and auxiliary officers of the territory of the court whenever these officers are appointed, promoted, transferred, retired, discharged, or granted leave of absence.

7. To hear the complaints referring to the administration of justice brought by the parties interested in causes on account of delay of proceedings; to adopt such measures which are within their power and to report these measures to the proper chamber whenever the gravity of the case requires it.

8. To appoint, besides the subordinate officers whose appointment is within their power according to law, the employees of the secretary's office, whose salaries are to be paid from the appropriation for material; to grant them leaves of absence, and to discharge them at will.

9. To adopt the measures that are necessary or convenient for keeping and preserving the archives and libraries of courts in good order.

10. To preside over chambers of justice, having the right of speech, no other person being allowed to speak without their permission, and to cause good order to be observed in the same.

11. To bring to the knowledge of the Government through the presiding judges of the territorial audiencia what they may consider necessary or convenient for a better administration of justice within their territory.

12. To receive the excuses for nonattendance of the associate justices and auxiliary and subordinate officers of the court and to cause those officers who are to replace them to be notified.

13. To make to the *fiscal* such indications as they may deem advisable for making the administration of justice more efficient without restricting the liberty of action which that officer enjoys. To communicate, whenever they consider such action necessary, to the *fiscal* of the territorial audiencia such matters as are considered to merit the notice of that officer concerning the manner in which the duties of the *fiscal* of the criminal audiencia are performed.

ART. 299. For the transaction of administrative affairs, criminal audiencias shall assemble in committee in the following cases:

1. To read orders not of a general character directed to the court or

to its presiding judge when their execution is incumbent upon the court.

2. To dispatch the reports which the Government or their hierarchical superiors request on matters which are attributed to the audiencias and which on account of their character do not belong to chambers of justice.

3. To exercise disciplinary jurisdiction in the cases provided for in this decree-law.

4. To discharge the other duties intrusted to them by the laws whenever they are not of a judicial character.

Chambers of administration shall convene regularly at least once a week on the day fixed for the purpose, and extraordinarily, whenever the presiding judge deems it necessary, and always before or after court hours.

The weekly session may be omitted only when there is no business pending. When the *fiscal* can not attend these meetings he shall be substituted by the person who is to serve in his place. These meetings shall exercise disciplinary jurisdiction over municipal judges or justices of the peace and judges of examination for offenses relating to their duties in criminal matters and over auxiliary officers of the court.

The disciplinary jurisdiction over associate justices of criminal audiencias and chambers shall belong to the chamber of administration of the supreme court.

ART. 300. In each territorial audiencia there shall be a criminal chamber, but it shall constitute together with the civil chamber only one court, composed of one presiding judge, one *fiscal*, and the presiding judges of chamber, associate justices, and auxiliary officers belonging to each one.

ART. 301. Criminal chambers of territorial audiencias may be divided, if the number of the personnel composing it so permits, into two or more sections, considered necessary in order to render the administration of justice more prompt.

ART. 302. Criminal chambers and audiencias shall administer justice ordinarily in the capital of their respective province, circumscription, or territory, but extraordinarily and accidentally they may, by decision of the presiding judge, convene in court in other towns in order to facilitate the holding of trials and securing the evidence which must be procured in connection with the latter.

ART. 303. The presiding judges of territorial audiencias shall order that the associate justices of the criminal audiencias of their territory render service by turn in other audiencias of the same, whenever the number of associate justices is incomplete and it is impossible to replace them by substitutes.

TITLE X.

COMPOSITION AND POWERS OF AUDIENCIAS.

ART. 304. Audiencias shall convene *in banc:*

1. To constitute themselves into chambers of justice.

2. For actions not having a judicial character.

ART. 305. Audiencias shall convene *in banc* as chambers of justice in the cases expressly established in this decree-law.

ART. 306. Whenever audiencias convene *in banc* as chambers of justice they shall conform to the provisions of law established with regard to the latter.

ART. 307. The presiding judges of audiencias shall appoint auxiliary and subordinate officers, respectively, who are to assist the court *in banc* resolved into a chamber of justice.

ART. 308. Audiencias may convene *in banc* for actions not of a judicial character in the following cases only:

1. To decide what may be proper with respect to the execution of the appointment of the various officers, to swear them in, and to give them possession of their respective offices.

2. To furnish the reports asked of them by the Government on legislative reforms, which are or should be applied by the judicial power, or on other points that bear a more or less direct relation to the administration of justice.

3. Whenever it is thus decided by the chamber of administration for deliberation on any serious matter.

4. Whenever for the same purpose the presiding judge issues orders to this effect.

ART. 309. For the sessions of the court *in banc* treated of in the foregoing article, all the associated justices shall be cited by order of the presiding judge with sufficient notice to give them time to attend.

The *fiscal* shall likewise be cited, who shall be represented by the *teniente fiscal* or by the person who acts as his substitute, whenever he is unable to attend for just cause.

ART. 310. The category and seniority of each associate justice shall determine the preference to be given him in the seats.

The *fiscal*, or the person attending as his substitute, shall occupy the place which is assigned him in the part treating on the department of public prosecution.

ART. 311. The *fiscal* shall have the right of argument and vote in a court *in banc*. The *teniente fiscal*, or the *abogado fiscal*, acting as his substitute, shall have the right of argument but no vote.

ART. 312. Persons directly or indirectly interested in the matters treated of can not be present at arguments and vote on the same.

ART. 313. Matters carried to the court *in banc* shall be prepared with a written report of the department of public prosecution.

Matters which on account of their urgency do not permit it, or on account of their ease of resolution or simplicity do not require it, in the opinion of the presiding judge, shall be excepted.

ART. 314. As a basis for the argument there shall serve the written decision of the *fiscal*, if there be any.

ART. 315. Arguments shall be held on each one of the questions presented to the court *in banc*, if there is anyone who desires to speak, and shall be closed only when no one desires to do so, or when on the motion of any associate justice, or of the presiding judge, the point is declared to have been argued sufficiently.

ART. 316. The right of speech shall be granted by turn in the order in which it is asked, those persons desiring to argue against the decision alternating with those who sustain it.

The *fiscal* shall not be obliged to await his turn.

ART. 317. When an associate justice requests that arguments be suspended, in order to make a more thorough study of the question in discussion, it shall be postponed to another session, if the urgency of the matter permits it.

ART. 318. In the cases in which the matter requires it, the presiding judge, in view of the arguments, shall appoint an associate justice or a committee composed of two or three associate justices to formulate a draft of a resolution, reporting on it at another session.

ART. 319. When the arguments on any matter have been closed, and neither a postponement has taken place nor a committee has been appointed according to the provisions of the two preceding articles, a vote shall be taken, beginning with the associate justice of lowest seniority and continuing by inverse order of seniority up to the presiding judge.

ART. 320. The associate justice who disagrees with the majority may ask that his vote appear in the minutes without necessity of explaining the same in writing, and his wish shall be complied with. When he desires to put his request in writing, he shall do so, stating his reasons, and this shall be inserted in the minutes, provided that he presents it within the day following that on which the resolution has been adopted.

ART. 321. The secretary of administration shall report on the matters brought before a court *in banc;* he shall be present during their argument and vote; he shall draw up the minutes of the proceedings, mentioning all resolutions and referring to the papers of the proceedings in which they are inserted; he shall make on the margin a note of the names of the persons who were present at the session; he shall keep the book of minutes and shall give the proper certifications in a proper case.

ART. 322. The presiding judge of his own accord, or at the instigation of the *fiscal*, or of any associate justice, may order the secretary to retire whenever such action is advisable on account of the special circumstances of the business or of the good name of the magistracy.

In the latter case the associate justice of lowest seniority shall perform the duties of secretary, and shall draft and authenticate the minutes.

ART. 323. There shall be two books of minutes:

One shall be called the "general book" of minutes, and shall be in charge of the secretary of administration, in which shall be entered all the proceedings and resolutions which are not of a confidential character.

Another, called the "private book". of minutes, in which shall be entered all resolutions of a confidential character. This book shall be in the custody of the presiding judge.

When, in the same session, matters of both kinds are treated of, each resolution shall be entered in its proper book.

The individual votes of associate justices shall be recorded in the book in which the corresponding resolution is entered.

TITLE XI.

CHAMBERS OF ADMINISTRATION OF AUDIENCIAS FOR ADMINISTRATIVE AFFAIRS.

ART. 324. It shall be the duty of chambers of administration of audiencies:

1. To supervise the administration of justice in their respective district, making use of the powers conferred on them by this decree-law and other special laws.

2. To transact business which is intrusted to them, and which on account of its special character does not come under the jurisdiction of chambers of justice.

3. To draft the reports requested of them by the Government, relating to the administration of justice, to the organization and administration of courts, and to the administrative and economical affairs of the same.

4. To draft the reports which, with relation to the subjects referred to in the preceding paragraph, are requested by their presiding judge.

5. To submit to the Government such recommendations which it may consider convenient or necessary with relation to the affairs referred to in the two preceding numbers.

6. To recommend to the Government the discharge of employees of the court who are of Royal appointment, and to decree their suspension when they consider it necessary.

With regard to auxiliary officers, the provisions of this decree-law with respect to their discharge shall be observed.

7. To decide the questions relating to the distribution of business among chambers of the court to which they belong, considering said questions as matters of internal administration and not of competency, and for this reason giving them only an administrative character and not a judicial character.

8. In cases of disagreement between associate justices or between chambers which may influence in the administration of justice, or in the order and good name of the courts, to adopt the prudent measures required by the case, and if these do not suffice, to make to the Government such recommendations as are thought to be most effective.

9. To exercise disciplinary jurisdiction in the cases mentioned in this decree-law.

10. To resolve into chambers of justice, in cases in which such action is ordered by this decree-law, or by other legal provisions.

11. To perform the other duties conferred upon them by this decree-law or other special provisions.

ART. 325. Chambers of administration shall convene at least once a week on the day assigned for the purpose, and extraordinarily whenever the presiding judge deems it necessary, and always before or after court hours.

The weekly session may be omitted only when there is no business pending.

ART. 326. Chambers of administration shall not be considered as legally constituted unless they are attended by all the persons who compose it, or in their default by those who should replace the officers that are absent or detained by some impediment.

ART. 327. In all matters referring to the manner of arguing and vote, to the books of minutes and of secret votes, and to the duties of the secretary, chambers of administration shall conform to the provisions of Title X that refer to meetings of superior courts *in banc.*

ART. 328. The resolutions of chambers of administration shall always state reasons.

When they conform with the opinion written by the *fiscal* and with the grounds on which he bases the same, it shall be sufficient for them to express their agreement in both respects.

ART. 329. Whenever chambers of administration resolve themselves into chambers of justice, or convene for the exercise of disciplinary jurisdiction, the department of public prosecution shall not form part thereof and shall limit itself to exercising the special duties of its office.

ART. 330. In matters taken cognizance of by chambers of administration resolved into courts of justice, they shall comply with the provisions of the laws of procedure.

TITLE XII.

MANNER OF CONSTITUTING INFERIOR COURTS AND CHAMBERS OF JUSTICE OF SUPERIOR COURTS.

FIRST AND LAST CHAPTER.

ART. 331. Superior and inferior courts shall hold public sessions on all days that are not holidays in the building designated for the purpose and during the time stated below:

Municipal judges or justices of the peace for the time necessary for the transaction of the business of the day. From this provision there shall be excepted those judges who perform their functions in towns with less than 500 inhabitants, who may assign only two days in a week for holding sessions, if they suffice for the transaction of their business.

Judges of first instance and examination for three hours at least.

Audiencias for four hours, of which three at least shall be devoted to the hearing of actions and causes.

ART. 332. Judges and presiding judges of courts shall designate the time hearings are to begin.

A placard constantly attached to the outside of the chambers of inferior or superior courts shall state the hour of opening.

ART. 333. No judge or associate justice shall fail to attend the audiencia without just cause.

ART. 334. Whenever a municipal judge or justice of the peace can not attend court, he shall notify his substitute sufficiently in advance in order that the court may be opened and the transaction of judicial business not suffer any delay.

If his failure to attend court exceeds five days, he shall inform the proper audiencia thereof.

ART. 335. Judges of the first instance or examination shall notify municipal judges or justices of the peace of the town in which they reside, in order that the latter may substitute them:

1. Whenever for any reason whatsoever they can not attend court.

2. Whenever they are obliged to leave the town of their residence in order to institute preliminary proceedings or other judicial actions.

3. When on account of a justifiable impediment they can not perform some judicial actions in the seat of the subdistrict.

ART. 336. When judges of first instance or examination can not hold public sessions for more than five days, they shall inform the proper audiencia thereof.

ART. 337. Associate justices who can not attend court for justifiable causes, shall inform the proper presiding judges thereof with sufficient notice, in order that the latter may, in a proper case, notify the persons who are to substitute them.

ART. 338. There shall be kept in audiencias a book of attendance, in which the secretary of administration shall make on each day of court sessions a note by chambers of the names of the associated justices who attended court, of those who are exempt from attending, and of those who have been excused, with a statement of the cause. The presiding judge of the court or the officer replacing him shall countersign these memoranda every day.

ART. 339. Three associate justices shall be sufficient to constitute a chamber in all cases in which the law does not require a fixed number of associate justices.

ART. 340. Associate justices of audiencias and presiding judges of chambers shall alternate among themselves, passing from one to the other whenever the service requires it. Every two years the colonial department, hearing the chambers of administration, may modify the distribution of associate justices in chambers.

ART. 341. Without prejudice to the provision of the preceding article, the secretary for the colonies may, on the recommendation of the respective chamber of administration, transfer associate justices of audiencias from one audiencia to another, provided that such action is suggested by the convenience of the service.

ART. 342. Whenever there is lacking in a chamber the number of associate justices necessary to constitute the same for hearing actions and causes, and that number must be completed with the superfluous ones of other chambers or with substitutes, in accordance with the provisions of this decree-law, the ordinary transaction of business or the hearings shall be suspended until the necessary number has been obtained.

ART. 343. The appointments of the persons assigned to attend a chamber other than that to which they belong, shall be immediately communicated to the persons designated, who shall excuse themselves, if, in the opinion of the presiding judge, there is a justifiable cause therefor.

When the presiding judge thinks that the reasons for non-attendance are sufficient, he shall appoint another associate justice, with respect to whom the provisions of the preceding article shall be observed.

. ART. 344. When the officers designated do not excuse themselves from attendance in civil matters, the solicitors of the parties shall be informed of their names, and the hearing shall be begun immediately, unless a challenge is made at once, even if verbal. In the latter case, after the challenge has been formulated in writing within the third day, the interlocutory issue of challenge shall be decided in the established form.

ART. 345. When no challenge having been made at once, and the hearing is proceeded with in accordance with the provisions of the preceding article, the discussion of the decision shall be suspended for three days. Substitute associate justices may be challenged within this time; after this period has elapsed, and no use of this privilege having been made, requests of challenges shall no longer be admitted, and the period assigned in which to render a decision shall be considered as begun.

ART. 346. If a challenge has been formulated and admitted as proper, the hearing shall remain without effect and shall take place again with associate justices of the chamber, or if it is not possible, the proceedings prescribed in articles 342, 343, 344, and in this article shall be again observed.

When a challenge is declared not well taken, a decision shall be pronounced by the associate justices who shall have attended the hearing, within the legal period, which shall begin on the day following the one on which a decision on the challenge is rendered.

Art. 347. In criminal causes, when the associate justices detailed to make up the required number do not form part of the regular personnel of the criminal chamber, their detail shall be communicated to the parties at least twenty-four hours before beginning the public trial. Challenges made after this time shall not be admitted.

Challenges made within the proper period shall be acted upon in the form prescribed.

TITLE XIII.

COURT SESSIONS AND POLICE OF INFERIOR AND SUPERIOR COURTS.

FIRST AND LAST CHAPTER.

Art. 348. Ordinary transaction of business and hearing of actions and causes shall take place in public.

Art. 349. Superior courts may, notwithstanding the provisions of the preceding article, order that the transaction of business and the hearing of actions and causes be made behind closed doors, in all cases in which such action is required by considerations of morality and decorum, at the request of one of the parties interested, at the instigation of the department of public prosecution, or of its own accord, before or during the hearing.

In the latter case the court shall order what is proper, after giving a brief hearing to the parties. There shall be no appeal from the decision.

Art. 350. Secretaries shall report the ordinary business in the order in which the petitions were presented in their respective offices.

Art. 351. Hearings of civil matters and of criminal causes shall be designated in the order of their conclusion.

From this provision shall be excepted questions of provisional maintenance, of competency, possessory injunctions, injunctions of new and injurious works, attachments, denial of judgment or proof, causes for crimes for which the law fixes a penalty greater than that of "presidio mayor," and other matters which by explicit prescriptions of other laws are given preference, which being concluded, shall be placed before the others for which a date has not yet been assigned.

Art. 352. Actions and causes shall be heard on the day assigned. If, at the conclusion of the hours of a court session, the hearing of any proceeding, action, or cause has not been concluded, it may be suspended to be continued on the following day or days, except when the presiding judge prolongs the session.

Art. 353. The hearing of civil matters may be suspended on the assigned day in the following cases only:

1. When it is prevented because of an action or a cause continued from the preceding day.

2. When for unforeseen reasons the number of associate justices required for a decision is lacking.

3. When it is requested by any of the parties, basing the request on the fact that their counsel has been prevented from appearing at the hearing, for a legitimate cause, in the opinion of the court.

ART. 354. Hearings of criminal causes may be suspended in the following cases only:

1. For any of the causes stated in No. 1 of the preceding article.

2. When, in criminal causes, an important witness is absent, or any steps to obtain proofs are wanting, on which, in the opinion of the court, its decision depends.

3. When the department of public prosecution, the defendant, or his counsel, or that of the accuser, in causes which can not be prosecuted officially, have been prevented from attending the hearing by legitimate causes.

ART. 355. When, without just cause, a lawyer who has been assigned by the court for the defense fails to attend, he shall be punished in a disciplinary manner.

ART. 356. A hearing which has been suspended shall be reassigned for the earliest date when the cause for suspension has disappeared, without prejudice in so far as possible to the order adopted for the hearing of other actions and causes.

The excess of costs occasioned by the suspension, for an unjustifiable failure to attend, of a litigant, the defendant, his counsel, the counsel of the accuser, in causes which can not be prosecuted officially, or of any important witness, shall always be charged to the person who has caused the same.

ART. 357. When, after a hearing has begun, any associate justice becomes sick or is prevented in any other manner from attending, and it is improbable that he will be able to attend after a few days, a new hearing shall be instituted, the number of associate justices being supplemented by the person or persons who should replace the absentee.

ART. 358. Parties to an action or a cause may, with the permission of the presiding judge, make such statements as they deem proper for their defense during the trial or when a petition is being presented in which they may be concerned.

The presiding judge must grant them the right of speech so long as they confine themselves to facts and preserve due decorum.

ART. 359. Visitors to court rooms shall remove their hats, remain silent, preserve good behavior, and observe the rules issued by the presiding officer for keeping order.

Associate justices, *fiscales*, and their auxiliary officers shall be respected in the same manner in any act or place in which they perform their respective duties.

ART. 360. Persons interrupting the hearing of any trial, cause, or other solemn judicial act, by showing ostentatiously their approval or disapproval, lacking the respect and consideration due courts, or in any way disturbing order, without, however, committing a crime by this action, shall be admonished at once by the presiding judge, and expelled from the court room if they disobey the first warning.

ART. 361. Persons resisting an order of expulsion shall be arrested and disciplined without appeal by a fine not exceeding 10 pesos in municipal courts or courts of justices of the peace, 15 pesos in courts of examination or of first instance, 20 pesos in criminal audiencias, and 30 pesos in territorial audiencias; and they shall not be released from arrest until they have paid the fine or otherwise have remained under arrest the number of days necessary to serve the sentence, computed at the rate of 2 pesos 50 centavos a day.

ART. 362. In the manner expressed in the preceding article, a punishment shall be imposed upon witnesses, experts, or any other persons who, either as parties or as their representatives, are guilty during hearings or solemn judicial acts, by speech, act, or writing, of lack of deference, respect, or obedience due courts, when such acts do not constitute crimes.

ART. 363. Persons who are subject to disciplinary jurisdiction in accordance with the provisions of this decree-law are not included in the provisions of the two preceding articles.

ART. 364. When the acts treated of in the two preceding articles are so serious as to be classed as crimes or offenses, their perpetrators shall be detained at once, the proper preliminary proceedings being instituted, and the prisoners being placed in the custody of the court of competent jurisdiction.

ART. 365. All judicial acts performed under the influence of intimidation or force shall be null.

Judges, superior courts, and chambers which have yielded to intimidation or force shall, as soon as they find themselves free therefrom, declare all acts performed under its influence null, and shall at the same time bring an action against the guilty parties.

TITLE XIV.

INSPECTION AND SURVEILLANCE OF THE ADMINISTRATION OF JUSTICE.

FIRST AND LAST CHAPTER.

ART. 366. The inspection and supervision of the duties of judges and superior courts shall be exercised:

By the presiding judges of superior courts.

By the chambers of administration of audiencias and of the supreme court.

By the chambers of justice of audiencias and of the supreme court.

By the courts of examination and of first instance.

ART. 367. The inspection and supervision shall be exercised by the presiding judge of the supreme court, and by presiding judges of audiencias, and by examining and first instance judges, by virtue of the powers and duties that are assigned to them.

ART. 368. In order to facilitate the inspection and supervision, annual statements of the civil and criminal matters pending or completed during the preceding judicial year shall be submitted:

By municipal courts or courts of justices of the peace to judges of examination and first instance.

By courts of examination and first instance to audiencias.

By audiencias to the supreme court.

ART. 369. The statements submitted by the judges of examination and first instance to the audiencias shall contain a summary of the ones they may have received from the municipal courts or from the courts of justices of the peace, besides their own, which it is their duty to forward.

The reports of the audiencias shall be accompanied by a summary of the statements of the municipal courts or courts of justices of the peace, and courts of examination and first instance.

ART. 370. In the supreme court a general summary of these statements shall be made and forwarded to the Government, together with those of the said court.

ART. 371. The regulations shall fix the form and the date on which each superior and inferior court must submit to their respective superior the statements referred to in the three preceding articles.

ART. 372. The presiding judge of the supreme court and the presiding judges of audiencias may order visits of inspection:

By order of the Government.

Officially.

At the instance of the department of public prosecution.

At the instance of chambers of administration.

At the instance of chambers of justice.

ART. 373. Judges of first instance and examination can not order visits of inspection of municipal courts or courts of justices of the peace; but when an inspection of any of said courts is necessary in their judgment, they shall communicate their opinion to the presiding judge of the audiencia, in order that the latter may decide what he may deem proper after hearing, in a proper case, the chamber of administration.

ART. 374. The chambers of administration may institute visits of inspection, whenever they consider it advisable, as a consequence of the memorials presented by judges of first instance or examination.

ART. 375. The chambers of justice shall make an inspection in the civil or criminal matters of which they take cognizance.

When in their judgment it would be advisable, in order to avoid abuses, to adopt some measure which does not lie within their power, or to make an inspection of some inferior or superior court, they shall state their opinion to the presiding judge, in order that the latter may decide what is proper after hearing the chamber of administration.

ART. 376. As visiting inspector there shall be selected an officer of a rank higher than that of the officers whose office is to be inspected.

ART. 377. The presiding judge of the supreme court may, whenever he considers such action proper, delegate to the presiding judge of an audiencia the appointment:

Of the associate justice to inspect a court of first instance.

Of the associate justice or judge of first instance to inspect municipal courts.

ART. 378. In the cases of delegation mentioned in the preceding article the judges and associate justices appointed for the inspection shall report to the presiding judges of the respective audiencia on all matters referring to the inspection.

ART. 379. In this service associate justices of audiencias shall serve by turn, without distinction between those composing the civil and criminal chambers. Presiding judges of audiencias and their chambers shall be exempted from this service. Excuses for exemption from this service shall not be accepted when not based on the impossibility to render it. Presiding judges of audiencias shall decide on said excuses according to their discretion, and shall submit them, with their own report containing a statement of reasons, to the colonial secretary.

ART. 380. The visits of inspection, made in conformity with the provisions of this title, shall include the examination of everything that refers to the rules established for the government of superior courts, and for a good administration of justice in the offices of their secretaries and in all their dependencies.

ART. 381. Visits of inspection in the cases expressly ordered by the presiding judges of audiencias or of the supreme court may include:

1. The civil registry.
2. The registry of property.
3. Registries of notarial offices.
4. The verification of the correctness of the annual reports.

ART. 382. The inspectors shall write a report of the inspection intrusted to them, which shall be forwarded to the *fiscal* of the court whose presiding judge may have ordered the visit.

ART. 383. The board of administration of the proper court, by virtue of the report of the *fiscal*, shall adopt such measures as lie within its power, and if it does not extend far enough it shall make such recommendations as it may consider proper to the Government.

ART. 384. The Government may appoint Royal commissaries to inspect superior and inferior courts whenever it considers such action necessary.

ART. 385. For the discharge of their duties, visiting inspectors shall be allowed a secretary and the other necessary employees, who shall be paid from the appropriations provided for these cases in the budgets of the respective island.

TITLE XV.

DISCIPLINARY JURISDICTION.

FIRST AND LAST CHAPTER.

ART. 386. The following officers shall be subject to disciplinary jurisdiction:

1. Judges and associate justices.
2. Auxiliary officers of inferior and superior courts.
3. Attorneys and solicitors.

ART. 387. Disciplinary jurisdiction over judges and associate justices shall be exercised:

By the judges of first instance over municipal judges or justices of the peace in a proper case.

By the chambers of administration of audiencias over judges of first instance and examination.

By the chamber of administration of the supreme court over associate justices.

The chambers of administration of audiencias and that of the supreme court, in order to exercise disciplinary jurisdiction, shall resolve themselves into chambers of justice.

ART. 388. The disciplinary jurisdiction shall not extend to acts or omissions which constitute a crime or to acts of private life which have not been publicly exposed.

ART. 389. Judges and associate justices shall be punished in a disciplinary manner:

1. When they show disrespect to their hierarchical superiors, either in speech, writing, or action.
2. When they show serious disregard of the respect due their equals.
3. When they trespass the reasonable limits of their authority with respect to the auxiliary and subordinate officers of inferior or superior courts, or with respect to those who assist them in judicial matters or those who attend the court-room, with whatever object it may be.
4. When they are negligent in fulfilling their duties.
5. When by the irregularity of their moral conduct or their bad habits which lower them in the public esteem, they affect the decorum of their office.
6. When, on account of expenditures beyond their means, they contract debts which result in writs of execution against them.
7. When they recommend to judges or superior courts matters pending in suits where the parties are present at the trial in criminal causes.
8. When they address to the executive power, to public officers, or to official corporations congratulations or censures for their actions.
9. When they take part, other than by casting their personal vote, in popular elections of the territory in which they perform their functions.

Notwithstanding this, they shall exercise the functions and fulfill the duties which are imposed upon them by virtue of their offices.

10. When they take part in meetings, manifestations, or other public acts of a political character, even if said acts are permitted to all other Spaniards.

11. When they attend *in corpore*, officially, or in ceremonial dress, feasts or public occasions, excepting only when it is their object to compliment the monarch or the regent of the realm, or when the Government gives explicit orders therefor.

12. When, without authorization from the colonial department, they publish writings defending their official conduct, or criticising that of other judges or associate justices.

ART. 390. Disciplinary penalties may be inflicted only:

By the presiding judges of the courts who have disciplinary jurisdic-. tion in the specific case.

By the *fiscales* of the same courts.

ART. 391. The presiding judges as well as the *fiscales* may inflict punishment by virtue of information of a positive character which has come to their knowledge; by complaint of the wronged parties, with sufficient facts to prove the existence of acts subject to disciplinary jurisdiction, or when they are notified by their hierarchical superiors.

ART. 392. The proceedings shall have merely the character of an examination, and shall consist of hearing the judge, or the associate justice and the *fiscal*, against whom charges are brought on the facts; of admitting evidence presented by both of them; of procuring the complement of the other evidence which may contribute to explain or prove the facts, and of receiving a written plea or argument from the party concerned and from the department of public prosecution.

ART. 393. The judge or the associate justice against whom said proceedings are directed shall be heard before the *fiscal* when the presiding judge has instituted the proceedings.

When the *fiscal* shall have instituted said proceedings, he shall be heard first.

The party whose papers are admitted in the hearing after those of the opponent, shall have the papers of the opponent submitted to him.

ART. 394. When the proceedings have been completed, the court or the chamber of administration shall either impose the disciplinary penalty or declare that there are no grounds for punishment.

ART. 395. The penalties imposed on municipal judges shall consist of only:

A simple reprimand.

A fine not less than 12 pesos nor more than 120 pesos.

ART. 396. The penalties imposed on judges of first instance and examination and associate justices shall consist of:

A simple reprimand.

A specific reprimand.

Postponement of promotion.

Loss of salary.

Suspension from office and loss of salary.

ART. 397. A simple reprimand shall consist of the literal communication of the penalty which the presiding judge of the court which imposed it shall make to the delinquent officer directly, if the latter is a municipal judge, judge of first instance and examination, or a presiding judge of an audiencia, and through the presiding judge of the proper court in all other cases.

ART. 398. The specific reprimand shall consist of a communication made in the manner specified in the preceding article, and of the loss of salary for a period of from one to three months.

ART. 399. The postponement of promotion shall consist of a deprivation of the right of promotion for a period of from six months to one year. This period shall be counted:

For strict seniority, from the day on which promotion would be due on account of the death of the person which causes a vacancy, or for any other reason.

For the promotions in which the appointment may be given to officers belonging to a particular part of the scale of service, or to the whole scale, from the day on which the sentenced officer acknowledges receipt of the communication informing him of the decision of the court.

ART. 400. The loss of salary shall last not less than three months nor more than six.

ART. 401. The penalty of suspension from employment and loss of salary shall last at least three months and may extend to twelve.

In cases of repetition of acts of the same kind by an officer who was punished for them previously with suspension from employment and loss of salary, said punishment shall always last one year.

ART. 402. Courts and chambers of administration may impose the penalties specified in the preceding article according to their good judgment, taking into account the greater or lesser gravity of the acts and omissions in question.

ART. 403. The penalties imposed upon municipal judges or justices of the peace and judges of first instance and examination may be appealed from to the chambers of administration of audiencias within the ten days following the one on which the sentence was communicated to the delinquent officers.

The chambers of administration, adding to the facts those that are presented or forwarded directly by the parties, shall confirm without the formality of a trial the sentence or penalty, if they consider it just; and otherwise they shall annul, mitigate, or increase it as they may deem proper.

ART. 404. The decisions of the chambers of administration of audiencias can not be appealed from.

ART. 405. Auxiliary officers of superior courts shall be punished in a disciplinary way, by judges of first instance and examination and by chambers of administration of audiencias, in the following cases:

When they are included in one of the cases specified in article 389 of this decree-law.

When they do not show due consideration to those who appeal to them in matters relating to their duties, and when they do not show themselves impartial in performing the same.

When they have vices which lower them in the public esteem.

ART. 406. Inferior courts shall exercise a disciplinary jurisdiction, in the cases specified in article 389, over the auxiliary officers who discharge their duties in said courts.

ART. 407. The penalties imposed upon auxiliary officers of inferior and of superior courts shall consist of—

Notice.

Warning.

A fine not exceeding 20 pesos in municipal courts or courts of justices of the peace; 40 pesos in courts of examination or first instance; 48 pesos in criminal audiencias, and 100 pesos in territorial audiencias.

A reprimand, behind closed doors, by the judge or by the presiding judge of the court in which the delinquent renders service.

A reprimand, behind closed doors, before the court or chamber to which the delinquent officer belongs.

Suspension from employment and loss of salary and emoluments for a period not to exceed six nor less than three months; in cases of repetition of acts of the same kind, this period may be extended to one year. During the suspension the salary and emoluments shall be paid to those who discharge their duties.

ART. 408. Auxiliary officers may appeal—

From the penalties imposed by municipal courts to courts of first instance or examination, against whose decision mitigating or increasing the penalty there shall be no further appeal.

From those imposed on their auxiliary officers by judges of first instance or examination, to chambers of administration of audiencias.

ART. 409. There shall be no further appeal from the penalties imposed by chambers of administration of audiencias.

ART. 410. In appeals entered before chambers of audiencias by auxiliary officers against the penalties imposed by municipal judges and judges of examination or of first instance, and against an appeal from said penalties when there are grounds therefor, the provisions of article 403 shall be observed in so far as they are applicable.

ART. 411. Attorneys and solicitors shall be punished in a disciplinary manner by municipal courts and by chambers of justice of all other courts, in the following cases:

When in the exercise of their profession they show, by work, writing, or act, a lack of the respect due inferior and superior courts.

When in defense of their clients they show a serious and unnecessary degree of incivility toward their colleagues.

When, after being called to order in oral allegations, they disobey the judge presiding over the court.

ART. 412. Notwithstanding the provisions of the foregoing article, they may, after having been called to order and after having asked and obtained permission from the judge or officer presiding over the act, explain the words they may have used and show the meaning or intention which they wished to convey, or fully apologize to the inferior or superior court.

ART. 413. The penalties imposed upon attorneys and solicitors shall always be imposed by the superior or inferior court or by the chamber of justice in which the proceedings giving rise to them have been had, or in which the proper decorum has not been observed in oral defenses.

ART. 414. Penalties shall be pronounced clearly, without taking into account more facts than appear in the documents or in the certificate which has been drawn up in the same proceedings by the secretary by order of the presiding judge, both with regard to the matter which is the object of the penalty as well as with reference to the explanations offered.

ART. 415. From the decisions in which municipal judges, judges of first instance and examination, and criminal audiencias have imposed penalties on attorneys or solicitors, appeals may be taken to territorial audiencias.

From the penalties imposed in chambers of justice of territorial audiencias a petition may be made only before the same chamber which has imposed said penalties.

ART. 416. The appeals and petitions referred to in the foregoing article shall be instituted in the manner established for interlocutory issues in civil matters.

ART. 417. The provisions of this title shall not interfere with the power of inferior or superior courts to impose on attorneys and solicitors the proper penalties, in accordance with the laws, for offenses and transgressions which are committed in the exercise of their duties, and which are not included in article 411.

TITLE XVI.

THE DEPARTMENT OF PUBLIC PROSECUTION.

ART. 418. The department of public prosecution shall see to the observance of this decree-law, shall institute judicial actions in matters relating to the public welfare, and shall act as the representative of the Government in its relations with the judicial power.

ART. 419. In all inferior and superior courts there shall be one or more representatives of the department of public prosecution.

ART. 420. The Government may increase the number of *abogados fiscales* whenever it is required by the service, and to reduce it when the service may be performed with a smaller number than that assigned at the proper time for each court.

In either case, an investigation shall be previously made, in which the chamber of administration and the *fiscal* of the respective court shall be heard.

In all cases the department of the treasury and of the colonies of the council of state shall be heard.

ART. 421. The *fiscales* of criminal audiencias shall submit the proper recommendations to territorial audiencias for the appointment of *fiscales* of municipal courts.

The *fiscales* of the territorial audiencias shall appoint directly the *fiscales* of municipal courts or of courts of justices of the peace, in the circumscription or the province of the criminal chamber, without necessity of recommendation, after receiving the reports from judicial and administrative authorities they may deem proper to request.

ART. 422. For selections, incapacities, excuses, claims, decisions of proceedings, filling of vacancies, and publication of appointments of *fiscales* of municipal courts or of courts of justices of the peace, and their substitutes, there shall be observed the provisions of this decree-law referring to municipal judges, with the following exception only:

The powers assigned to and duties imposed on presiding judges of audiencias shall be considered as assigned to and imposed on the *fiscales* of the same.

ART. 423. Wherever *promotores fiscales* do not exist, the *fiscales* of municipal courts who are lawyers shall represent the department of public prosecution in all matters in which the latter should be heard, in accordance with the law of criminal procedure or any other laws.

The *fiscales* of audiencias, notwithstanding this provision, no matter whether the *fiscales* of municipal courts or of courts of justices of the peace are lawyers or not, may make use of their auxiliary officers, or appoint lawyers to discharge the duties of the department of public prosecution in the matters referred to in the foregoing paragraph, or examine personally the proceedings in progress in courts of first instance and examination.

The lawyers discharging said duties shall receive the same remuneration as is given to substitutes.

ART. 424. The appointments of officers of the department of public prosecution in the various cases shall be made in accordance with the provisions contained in chapter 2, title 3, of this decree-law.

CHAPTER II.

GENERAL CONDITIONS FOR ALL OFFICES OF THE DEPARTMENT OF PUBLIC PROSECUTION.

ART. 425. To the persons filling offices of the department of public prosecution, of whatsoever rank or category, there shall be extended all the provisions established in articles 73 to 79 for judicial officers in matters referring to qualifications, incapacity, absolute or relative incompatibility, and exemption from obligatory duties.

ART. 426. The incompatibilities established in article 80 shall likewise be extended to the proper officers of the department of public prosecution.

From the provisions of the preceding paragraph there shall be excepted:

1. The *fiscales* of municipal courts or courts of justices of the peace and their substitutes.

2. The substitutes of *abogados fiscales* of audiencias.

3. Persons rendering service in the department of public prosecution accidentally or provisionally.

4. Persons discharging duties of the department of public prosecution in Habana.

The prohibitive provisions established for judicial officers in article 82 shall include the persons obtaining appointments in the department of public prosecution, in the same superior courts, and within the same territory. Persons violating these provisions shall incur the penalty fixed in article 83. From this provision there shall be excepted the officers that are included in the first three numbers of the foregoing article.

ART. 427. Persons appointed to offices of the department of public prosecution can not practice law. From this provision there shall be excepted only those mentioned in the first three numbers of article 426.

ART. 428. In order to hold office in the department of public prosecution, it shall be necessary, besides possessing the qualifications prescribed in article 73, to be a licentiate at law, graduated from a university supported by the State. From this provision there shall be excepted only the *fiscales* of municipal courts or of courts of justices of the peace.

CHAPTER III.

SPECIAL QUALIFICATIONS OF FISCALES OF MUNICIPAL COURTS OR OF COURTS OF JUSTICES OF THE PEACE.

ART. 429. The *fiscales* of municipal courts or of courts of justices of the peace and their substitutes shall possess the qualifications which are required of municipal judges or justices of the peace according to article 84.

ART. 430. The preference granted to lawyers over persons who are not such, applicable, according to article 85, to municipal courts or courts of justices of the peace, shall be extended to the offices of *fiscales* of the same, provided there are no reasons to the contrary. In this case, their not having reached the age of twenty-five shall not be an obstacle.

Chapter IV.

OATHS AND TAKING POSSESSION OF OFFICE BY OFFICERS OF THE DEPARTMENT OF
PUBLIC PROSECUTION.

Art. 431. Officers of the department of public prosecution, in taking possession of office, shall be formally sworn in, in the same manner as judicial officers, swearing:

To observe and cause to be observed the Constitution of the Monarchy.

Allegiance to the King.

To promote the administration of justice.

To carry out all the laws and regulations referring to the duties of their office.

Art. 432. The *fiscales* of the audiencia of Habana, of territorial and of criminal audiencias, shall be sworn in and shall take possession of their offices before their respective courts, in the presence of the judges of first instance, examining judges, and municipal judges of the town, and the auxiliary and subordinate officers of the audiencias.

The *tenientes fiscales* of the said audiencias, with the exception of those of criminal audiencias, shall be sworn in and shall take possession of their offices in the same manner as the associate justices of the same.

The *abogados fiscales* of the said audiencias and the *tenientes fiscales* of criminal audiencias shall be sworn in before the chamber of administration of the respective territorial audiencia, taking possession before the proper court.

Art. 433. The provisions of this decree-law referring to the swearing in of municipal judges or of justices of the peace and their taking possession of office shall apply also to the representatives of the department of public prosecution in the said courts.

Chapter V.

DATES AND POSTPONEMENT OF EMBARKATION AND OF TAKING PERSONAL POSSESSION
OF OFFICE.

Art. 434. The rules established in this decree-law for judicial officers with reference to dates, postponements of embarkation, and taking personal possession of office, shall be applicable to the officers of the department of public prosecution.

Chapter VI.

SENIORITY, PRECEDENCE, TITLES, AND DRESS OF OFFICERS OF THE DEPARTMENT OF
PUBLIC PROSECUTION.

Art. 435. In order to compute the seniority of officials of the department of public prosecution, the same rules shall be observed as are established in this decree-law in the various cases for judicial officers.

ART. 436. The *fiscales* of audiencias, in sessions *in banc* and in chambers of administration, shall be given a place and seat among the presiding judges of chambers, preserving among these officers the place that belongs to them by right of seniority, without any discrimination because of the office which they respectively hold.

ART. 437. The *tenientes fiscales* of audiencias, when attending sessions *in banc* and chambers of administration, the respective *fiscal* being prevented from attending, shall occupy the place and seat from the right after the last associate justice.

When the *fiscal* and the *teniente fiscal*, being prevented from attending, are substituted by the *abogado fiscal*, the latter shall occupy the place and seat after the last associate justice from the left.

ART. 438. In chambers of justice the *fiscales* of audiencias shall have a seat at the right side of the court table.

The *tenientes fiscales* and the *abogados fiscales*, when performing the duties of their offices, shall take seats at the left side.

ART. 439. Greater seniority shall give right of precedence—

1. In the order of seats and places among officers belonging to the same category.

2. When the *abogados fiscales* are substitutes for the *tenientes fiscales*.

3. When the *fiscales* attend chambers of administration, in cases of vacancies, or of any impediment of the *fiscales* and the *tenientes fiscales*.

ART. 440. The officers of the department of public prosecution shall have the same title as is given to their equals in the judicial service.

ART. 441. The provisions of articles 132, 133, 134, and 135 of this decree-law, referring to officers of the judicial service, are applicable also to officers of the department of public prosecution.

ART. 442. The *fiscales* of municipal courts or of courts of justices of the peace, on official or formal occasions, while attending as such, shall wear a medal similar to that prescribed for municipal judges, made according to a model which is or may be hereafter prescribed, and bearing the following inscription: "Ministerio fiscal" (department of public prosecution).

ART. 443. The other officers of the department of public prosecution, of whatsoever class and category, shall wear ceremonial dress on the occasions referred to in article 137 of this decree-law.

The ceremonial dress of the other officers of the department of public prosecution of the various ranks shall be the same as that used by the judges and associate justices with whom they are respectively equal in rank.

ART. 444. The prohibition of article 139 of this decree-law shall be extended to the department of public prosecution.

ART. 445. The reverse of the medals used by the officers of the department of public prosecution shall bear "Ministerio fiscal" (department of public prosecution) instead of the word "Justicia" (justice). ·

ART. 446. The officers of the department of public prosecution shall receive the following yearly salaries:

The *promotores fiscales* of the entrance category, 600 pesos as pay and 900 pesos as extra pay.

The *promotores fiscales* of the promotion category, 750 pesos as pay and 1,125 pesos as extra pay.

The *promotores fiscales* of the final category and the *abogados fiscales* of criminal audiencias, 900 pesos as pay and 1,350 pesos as extra pay.

The *abogados fiscales* of territorial audiencias and the *tenientes fiscales* of criminal audiencias, 1,100 pesos as pay and 1,660 pesos as extra pay.

The *abogados fiscales* of the audiencia of Habana and the *tenientes fiscales* of territorial audiencias, 1,400 pesos as pay and 2,100 pesos as extra pay.

The *fiscales* of criminal audiencias, 1,700 pesos as pay and 2,550 pesos as extra pay.

The *fiscales* of territorial audiencias and the *teniente fiscal* of the audiencia of Habana, 2,000 pesos as pay and 3,000 pesos as extra pay.

The *fiscal* of the audiencia of Habana, 2,300 pesos as pay and 3,550 pesos as extra pay.

ART. 447. The *tenientes fiscales* and the *abogados fiscales* who leave the place of their residence to attend extraordinary chambers of audiencias, shall receive an extra pay of 5 pesos for each day spent away from their place of residence.

This increase shall not be computed for retired pay.

CHAPTER VIII.

TRANSFERS, SUSPENSIONS, DISCHARGES, AND RETIREMENTS OF OFFICERS OF THE DEPARTMENT OF PUBLIC PROSECUTION.

ART. 448. Transfers, suspensions, discharges, and retirements of officers of the department of public prosecution shall be made in every respect in accordance with the form and rules established in Title IV of this decree-law for officers of the judicial service.

CHAPTER IX.

LIABILITY OF OFFICERS OF THE DEPARTMENT OF PUBLIC PROSECUTION.

ART. 449. There may be demanded of officers of the department of public prosecution a liability, civil as well as criminal, in the cases and in the manner established in Title V of this decree-law, without further modifications than those mentioned in the following articles.

ART. 450. A trial for criminal liability may be instituted only by virtue of a ruling of the competent superior court or at the instance of the department of public prosecution.

ART. 451. Courts before officially proceeding against officers of the department of public prosecution shall grant a hearing to the immediate hierarchical superior of said officers, communicating to him the facts on which the cause is to be based.

CHAPTER X.

POWERS OF THE DEPARTMENT OF PUBLIC PROSECUTION.

ART. 452. It shall be the duty of the department of public prosecution:

1. To see to the carrying out of the laws, regulations, ordinances, and provisions of an obligatory character referring to the administration of justice, and to require their observance.

2. To give to its respective subordinates the general or special instructions for the fulfillment of their duties, with the aim of making the service of the department as uniform as possible.

3. To preserve intact the powers and competency of superior and inferior courts in general, to defend the same from any invasion coming either from the judicial or the administrative service, raising questions of competency, appeals on account of abuses of jurisdiction, or appeals from wrongs of ecclesiastical courts (recursos de fuerza en conocer) and opposing questions of competency that are raised unjustly against the inferior or superior courts in which the officers of said department discharge their duties.

4. To represent the State, the Administration, and public educational and benevolent institutions in questions in which they are a party, either as plaintiffs or as defendants.

5. To take part in an official capacity in causes concerning the civil status of persons.

6. To represent and defend minors, incapacitated persons, absentees, or persons prevented from administering their property, until guardians have been selected for the protection of their property and rights.

7. To promote the institution of criminal causes, for crimes and offenses, whenever their perpetration comes to the knowledge of the officers of the department; if said causes have not been begun *ex officio* by the proper officers.

8. To appear for the Government in all criminal causes, with the exception only of those which, according to the laws, may only be instituted at the instigation of the aggrieved party.

9. To investigate with special diligence arbitrary arrests that are made and to see to their punishments.

10. To attend hearings in matters in which the department constitutes a party, with the exception of such matters only in which the Government can not be represented.

11. To raise questions of disciplinary punishment in cases in which such action is proper according to the laws.

12. To see to the fulfillment of decisions in actions and causes in which the department acts as a party, and to this effect officers of the department shall have the right and obligation to visit penal institutions, to see whether sentences of criminal causes are being executed in the form imposed.

They shall not, nevertheless, introduce changes in the management and discipline of prisons, confining themselves, in a proper case, to informing the Government of the defects which they have noticed and the means of correcting them.

13. To bring to the knowledge of the supreme court and of the Government serious abuses and irregularities noticed in inferior and superior courts, when the department has no power to remedy them in any other way.

14. To express verbally an opinion in urgent matters of easy solution which shall be stated in the ruling or decree pronounced in the matter.

15. To request of inferior courts and the superior court of the territory in which officers of the department render service, and which are subordinate to the court to which they belong, causes and matters that have been terminated, in order to exercise supervision over the administration of justice, and to demand the correction of abuses that may occur.

16. To request assistance from the authorities, of whatsoever class they may be, for the discharge of the duties of the department, said authorities being responsible according to law for the consequences resulting from their failure or negligence in rendering said assistance.

17. To fulfill the other obligations imposed upon the department by the laws.

ART. 453. *Fiscales* shall adopt such rules as they think proper for the distribution of the work among the *tenientes fiscales* and the *abogados fiscales* who are under their immediate orders, preserving equality of work among them.

ART. 454. The *fiscales* of the respective audiencias shall appoint substitute *abogados fiscales* to replace the regular officers in cases of vacancies or any other impediment.

ART. 455. Lawyers appointed as substitutes shall have a right to the same benefits that are granted to substitute associate justices.

The same rights shall be enjoyed by the *fiscales* of municipal courts or courts of justices of the peace who are lawyers.

CHAPTER XI.

UNITY AND DEPENDENCE OF THE DEPARTMENT OF PUBLIC PROSECUTION.

ART. 456. In order to maintain the unity and dependence of the department of public prosecution, the *fiscales* of territorial audiencias shall have the power of inspection over each and all the *fiscales* of the criminal audiencias of the respective territory, for which purpose the latter shall submit to them within the first fifteen days of the month of May of each year a memorial on the administration of justice in criminal matters in the audiencia of their circumscription; and the *fiscales* of territorial audiencias on said reports shall make such observations as they deem proper to the *fiscales* of criminal audiencias submitting said reports, and shall give account of this action to the *fiscal* of the supreme court, submitting to him another memorial during the first fifteen days of July.

During the judicial year, the *fiscales* of territorial audiencias may likewise request of those of criminal audiencias the data and information they may deem proper, and adopt appropriate measures in order to maintain the unity of jurisprudence, bringing all matters to the knowledge of the *fiscal* of the supreme court.

ART. 457. The *fiscal* of the supreme court is the chief of the department of public prosecution in the entire Monarchy.

The *fiscales* of territorial audiencias are chiefs of the department of public prosecution in their respective territory; but in criminal trials they shall only exercise the duties of their office before the criminal chamber of the respective territorial audiencia or before the same audiencia *in banc*, when the latter resolves itself into a chamber of justice.

The *fiscales* of criminal audiencias are chiefs of officers representing the department of public prosecution in municipal courts.

The *fiscal* of the supreme court shall have disciplinary jurisdiction over all the officers of the department of public prosecution.

The *fiscales* of territorial audiencias shall have disciplinary jurisdiction over those serving under their immediate orders and over the *fiscales* of criminal audiencias.

The latter over their auxiliary officers and over the *fiscales* of municipal courts in their province or circumscription.

Officers sentenced to a punishment by the *fiscales* of territorial audiencias or by those of criminal audiencias, may enter an appeal to the *fiscal* of the supreme court, and, as a last resort, to the Secretary for the colonies.

Officers sentenced to a punishment by the *fiscal* of the supreme court may appeal only to the said secretary.

ART. 458. As a consequence of the provisions of the foregoing article every *fiscal:*

1. Shall report to his immediate superior the crimes and offenses of which he has knowledge brought either at the instigation of the aggrieved party, or *ex officio*, or at his request. He shall do this in the time and manner prescribed by the laws, regulations, or by the rulings of his hierarchical superiors.

2. Shall conform to the instructions communicated to him by his hierarchical superiors in matters referring to duties of the department of public prosecution.

3. Shall consult his immediate hierarchical superiors, whenever such

action is necessary or advisable on account of the gravity of the matter, the difficulty of the case, or for any other reason.

4. Shall respectfully submit to his hierarchical superiors such observations as he thinks advisable, relating to the orders and instructions which he considers contrary to law, or which, on account of erroneous construction or any other reason, are inadmissible; he shall not, however, deviate from said orders and instructions until he receives an order to this effect from his superior.

5. Shall enter in the proper time and form, when not instructed to the contrary, appeals proper in matters in which he takes part, without prejudice to what his superior may decide as to their prosecution.

ART. 459. For the execution of the provisions of the two last numbers of the preceding article the superior, in accepting observations submitted by his subordinate, when he finds said observations legal and well taken, shall modify or countermand the orders and instructions which he himself may have issued.

In case said orders have come from another hierarchical superior, the superior referred to in the preceding paragraph shall bring said observations to the knowledge of the former, giving at the same time his own information, which he considers proper, in order that the matter may be decided in a proper manner.

When the orders and instructions have been given by the Government he shall report to it in order that the latter may decide on the matter.

ART. 460. When the superior does not consider the observations submitted by his subordinate as legal or well taken, he shall give him such instructions as he deems fit; and if he thinks such action advisable, he may appoint another of his subordinates to substitute him in the dispatch of the affairs.

CHAPTER XII.

DISCIPLINARY PUNISHMENT OF OFFICERS OF THE DEPARTMENT OF PUBLIC PROSE-
CUTION.

ART. 461. In cases which, according to article 389, the disciplinary punishment of judges and associate justices is proper, it may also give occasion to disciplinary punishment of officers of the department of public prosecution.

ART. 462. The disciplinary penalties that shall be imposed on officers of the department of public prosecution shall be the ones fixed in article 368 for judges and associate justices.

ART. 463. The disciplinary penalties may be imposed after examining the officers concerned—

By the *fiscal* of the supreme court on all officers of the department of public prosecution.

By *fiscales* of audiencias on the officers serving under their immediate orders and on those of municipal courts or courts of justices of the peace and courts of first instance and examination.

ART. 464. From the disciplinary penalties imposed by *fiscales* of audiencias an appeal lies to the *fiscal* of the supreme court.

From the penalties imposed by the *fiscal* of the supreme court, either directly or by confirming, modifying, or revoking the penalties imposed by *fiscales* of audiencias, an appeal lies only to the colonial department.

ART. 465. There shall be no further appeal from the decisions of the colonial department.

TITLE XVII.

ATTORNEYS AND SOLICITORS.

CHAPTER I.

PROVISIONS COMMON TO ATTORNEYS AND SOLICITORS.

ART. 466. In towns which have territorial audiencias there shall be an association of attorneys (*colegio de abogados*) and an association of solicitors (*colegio de procuradores*), the principal object of which shall be the equal distribution of duties among those practicing in the courts of the locality, the good order of the respective corporation, and the decorum, fellowship, and discipline of the members.

ART. 467. Associations of attorneys and solicitors may also be established:

In the capitals of provinces where there is no territorial audiencia.

In towns in which there are 20 practicing solicitors or attorneys.

ART. 468. For eligibility to membership of the association of attorneys, those shall be considered as residents who, without staying in the town, reside and practice their profession within a radius of two leagues, provided that said attorneys agree to share with other members in due proportion the duties imposed upon them.

This rule does not include solicitors who must necessarily reside where the association is situated.

ART. 469. The membership of these associations shall be unlimited, and all candidates requesting admission shall be admitted, provided they prove that they possess the legal capacity prescribed by this decree-law for practicing the respective profession.

ART. 470. The by-laws of the associations of solicitors and attorneys shall establish their organization and management, the conditions of admission, the relations of members with the association and with courts, the obligations of the former, and the disciplinary penalties which may be incurred in matters not appertaining to the disciplinary jurisdiction of inferior and superior courts.

ART. 471. No person can practice the profession of attorney and that of solicitor at the same time.

The person who, after practicing one of said professions, selects the other shall cease to practice the former, and shall be dropped from the list of the respective association.

ART. 472. In the towns that have associations of attorneys or solicitors these professions can be practiced only by those who are members of said associations and have offices in the said towns.

Persons who do not have the necessary qualifications for the profession of attorneys and of solicitors can not be admitted as members of the associations.

ART. 473. Attorneys and solicitors shall be obliged to defend the poor free of charge, the conditions established in this decree-law being observed, in order that this obligation be not distributed unequally.

ART. 474. The governing boards of associations of attorneys and solicitors shall respectively establish such rules as they consider most just for turns in distribution of actions and causes of indigents, preserving the strictest possible equality.

The deans of the associations shall make appointments in conformity with said rules.

ART. 475. In towns that are seats of judicial subdistricts, in which there are no associations of attorneys, the secretary of the court of first instance and examination, under the supervision of the judge, shall make the distribution of actions and causes of indigents among the solicitors and attorneys, observing the strictest possible equality.

ART. 476. Where there is no association of solicitors or attorneys, it shall be necessary in order to practice these professions:

1. To possess the qualifications required therefor by this decree-law.

2. To belong to or be a resident of the town in which the law office is to be opened, and in the town of the residence of the court at which he practices the profession of solicitor.

3. To register in the inferior or superior court as a practicing attorney.

4. To pay the tax of industrial subsidy.

ART. 477. Solicitors and attorneys before beginning the practice of their profession shall take an oath to observe the constitution of the Monarchy, to be faithful to the King, and to carry out strictly and loyally all the obligations imposed on them by the laws and provisions of regulations.

ART. 478. The oath referred to in the preceding article shall be taken:

In towns where there is a territorial audiencia, before the chambers of administration of the same.

Where there is a criminal audiencia, before the same.

Where there is no criminal audiencia, before a judge of first instance and examination, if there be any, and if not, before a municipal judge.

ART. 479. Attorneys and solicitors shall be subject to the disciplinary jurisdiction of courts in the terms fixed by this decree-law.

ART. 480. Attorneys desiring to practice their profession in the colonial provinces and possessions shall present their degrees duly legalized or accompanied with a certificate of identity issued by the colonial department.

CHAPTER II.

PRACTICING ATTORNEYS.

ART. 481. The following are the requirements for practicing the legal profession:

1. To be at least 21 years of age.
2. To be a licentiate at law.
3. Not to have been prosecuted criminally.
4. Not to have been sentenced to corporeal punishment, or to have been exonerated therefrom.

ART. 482. The following persons can not practice the legal profession:

1. Persons discharging judicial duties or the duties of the department of public prosecution.

From this rule are excepted municipal judges or justices of the peace, and *fiscales* of municipal courts or courts of justices of the peace.

2. Persons filling offices in the service of the general administration of the State.

3. Auxiliary officers and employees of courts.

ART. 483. Notwithstanding the provisions of articles 472 and 476, lawyers who are not registered in the associations as having law offices, or in the inferior or superior courts to practice law, but who possess the qualifications specified in article 481, may defend either in writing or orally their own civil matters or criminal cases, and those of their relatives within the fourth degree of consanguinity or second of affinity.

In these cases, wherever there is an association of attorneys, they shall be qualified by its dean. Where there is none, they shall present proofs of their being attorneys and of their relationship, in a proper case, to the judge or court before whom or in which they are to act in defense, and said judge or court shall grant them their authorization.

ART. 484. Attorneys of an association in a capital of an audiencia may act in defense before the ordinary and extraordinary chambers of the same in whatever towns said chambers are convened.

ART. 485. Attorneys who shall act in defense of indigents can not excuse themselves from this obligation in criminal cases without personal and justifiable reasons, which shall be ruled upon by Deans of associations, where there are any, according to their good judgment, and in their absence by the judge or courts before which said defense should be made.

ART. 486. Attorneys shall appear before courts in the dress of the profession, which shall be black, with a cap and gown, of the same kind as those of judges and associate justices, and without any other distinctive mark whenever they attend solemn acts and hearings of inferior or superior courts.

Chapter III

SOLICITORS.

ART. 487. In order to be a solicitor, it is necessary:

1. To prove an expert knowledge in the order and procedure of trials and in the obligations imposed upon their profession by law.

This qualification shall be proved in the manner established in the regulations.

From this formality are excepted those who are attorneys or who have completed the studies and obtained the qualification required for the office of notary.

2. To possess the qualifications established for attorneys in numbers 1, 3, and 4, of article 481.

3. In cases of persons who shall select the profession hereafter, by virtue of this decree-law, to constitute as a guaranty, a deposit in specie or in paper currency of the State, at the rate of the official quotation to the amount fixed below:

Five thousand pesos in Habana.

One thousand five hundred pesos in other cities having a territorial audiencia.

One thousand pesos in localities having a criminal audiencia.

Five hundred pesos in localities having a court of examination or of first instance.

Two hundred in other localities.

This security may be given on real estate of three times the value fixed in the preceding scale.

In every case the guaranty may consist of one-fifth of the sums fixed, adding to it the title of an alienated office of that class while it shall not have reverted to the State.

ART. 488. The bonds of solicitors shall serve as security for fines imposed upon them, for money received from their clients for judicial costs, or in any other civil, criminal, or disciplinary liability arising in the practice of their profession.

ART. 489. Whenever the bond is reduced for any of the causes expressed above, it must be completed by the solicitor. If he fails to complete it within two months, he shall be suspended from his office.

ART. 490. Whenever a solicitor ceases to perform his duties for any reason whatsoever, an announcement shall be published in the official newspaper of the province in which said solicitor had his office and in the official newspapers of the town, should there be any, in order that any claims against him may be made within the period of six months.

After said period has elasped, the deposit shall be returned to the solicitor if there are no claims.

If just claims have been made within the proper time the creditors shall receive from the deposit what is due them.

ART. 491. Solicitors of the same town shall replace one another in cases of leave of absence, sickness, or any other legitimate impediment.

In towns not having a number of solicitors sufficient to represent the parties or to replace one solicitor by another, the judicial authority may appoint temporarily a person who, besides the necessary conditions of age and morality, possesses knowledge enabling him to act as solicitor, it being understood that this appointment shall always be special and for a certain case.

ART. 492. Solicitors are absolutely forbidden to perform auxiliary duties in the dependencies of inferior or of superior courts.

TITLE XVIII.

RECESSES, LEAVES, AND COMMISSIONS OF THE SERVICE.

CHAPTER I.

DAYS ON WHICH COURTS DO NOT HOLD SESSIONS.

ART. 493. Superior and inferior courts shall not hold sessions:

1. On whole holidays.
2. On the King's day, and on those of the Queen, the Regent of the Realm, and the Prince of Asturias.
3. On Thursday and Friday of Holy Week.
4. On national holidays.

ART. 494. Without prejudice to the provisions of the preceding article, the days specified therein shall be juridical days for the institution of preliminary proceedings in criminal causes, without being specially made such, and may be made such for any other urgent, civil, or criminal proceedings.

ART. 495. For the purposes of the preceding article, such proceedings shall be considered as urgent the postponement of which may, in the judgment of the judge or court, cause great damage to the defendants, the litigants, or to the good administration of justice.

CHAPTER II.

LEAVES.

ART. 496. Municipal judges of the Antilles and justices of the peace of the Philippines may absent themselves for eight days or less from the municipal territory in which they reside, leaving their substitute in charge of their offices, and informing the judge of first instance of the subdistrict of the fact.

In order to absent themselves for more than eight and less than thirty days they must obtain, in writing, leave from the judge of first instance of the subdistrict, and for a period of from thirty to ninety days from the presiding judge of the audiencia.

ART. 497. In none of the cases referred to in the two preceding articles may municipal judges or justices of the peace absent themselves from the municipal territory in which they perform their duties until the respective substitute takes charge of his office.

ART. 498. Neither judges of examination nor of first instance may absent themselves without leave from the districts in which they render service; nor associate justices of whatsoever rank from localities where the courts to which they belong are situated.

From the provisions of the preceding paragraph shall be excepted those who are absent in order to perform their duties or to take some legal steps in the administration of justice.

ART. 499. No leave shall be granted except upon the request of an employee, passed upon by his immediate superior. If it is made on account of ill health, it must be duly proven. If it is made on account of personal matters, the immediate superior, in passing upon it, shall state whether the granting of the leave would cause injury to the public service.

It shall be an obligation to grant leaves when the person interested in soliciting the same has complied with the requirements of the preceding paragraph.

ART. 500. The granting of leaves shall be made in conformity with the following rules:

1. It shall be an indispensable condition for requesting leaves to have remained without interruption in active service for three consecutive years in any of the colonial provinces.

2. The maximum period of leaves, which can not be extended, shall be regulated as follows:

Six months for officers of the Philippine Islands and four for those of the islands of Cuba and Puerto Rico, who have fulfilled the conditions established in the preceding rule; nine months and six months, respectively, for officers of the said islands, if they have remained in the condition established by rule 1 for six consecutive years; twelve months and eight months, respectively, for officers of said islands, if their uninterrupted active service has reached the period of ten years.

3. Making use of leaves, on whatever condition they may have been granted, deprives the officer of the privilege of requesting another until the conditions which, according to the case, are specified in rules 1 and 2 shall have been again fulfilled.

4. Leaves shall be requested by the officers concerned of the colonial department, in due form and through the proper channel.

5. Only in case of serious sickness, duly proved, and which endangers the life of the officers interested, may governors-general grant leaves for Europe, for half the time, respectively, fixed in rule 2, after a proper investigation, instituted by the immediate superiors of the officers.

6. Both in making investigations to prove the causes for which leave is asked and in the payment of salary during the said leave, according to whether it has been granted on account of sickness or for personal matters, there shall be taken into account the provisions of the preceding rule, and further that it is obligatory to grant every leave in

which the officer requesting it has proved his ill health, and that such officer shall draw only the personal salary assigned to his office from the day on which he ceases to perform his duties until the day on which he resumes them.

ART. 501. Leaves for any point of Asia or America not included in the colonial provinces shall be granted by governors-general for the period of forty-five days, an extension being limited to twenty-two days more, in cases of sickness that has been proved, the officers on such leaves drawing the pay and the extra pay corresponding to their office.

When leaves are granted for personal matters, they shall in no case exceed forty-five days, during which the officer on leave shall not draw any pay whatsoever.

ART. 502. Leaves for the interior of the islands in which the officers of the judicial and of the public prosecution services fill offices shall be granted by the proper superior authorities in conformity with the following rules:

1. Employees of the said services can not absent themselves from the town in which they perform their special duties without leave granted by the proper authority. An officer absenting himself without leave shall be considered as resigning his office, and shall be declared suspended, this provision being without prejudice to the other liabilities that may arise.

2. Leaves must be asked for in writing and through the immediate superior. If they are made on account of ill health, it is necessary to justify the request by a medical certificate.

If the justification presented by the petitioner appears insufficient, in the opinion of his chief, the latter may order that they be amplified.

In a petition for leave the employee presenting it shall state the leaves he has enjoyed during the three preceding years.

3. Immediate superiors, in passing upon requests for leaves, shall inform themselves as to the necessity for said leaves to employees, and as to the possibility of granting them without prejudice to the service.

4. Leaves in case of sickness shall be granted with full salary for one month only, and with half salary for fifteen days more; those granted for other reasons shall be without salary.

5. Leaves taken by employees shall be noted in their record of service and in their personal record.

6. An employee who has obtained leave during three consecutive years shall not obtain another one during the next three years.

ART. 503. A leave granted an employee shall be null if, before making use of it, the employee is transferred to another office, a new order being required in order that he may make use of the same in his new position.

ART. 504. A report shall be made to the colonial department on every leave granted to said employees in order that a memorandum of it may be made in the respective personal record

ART. 505. The period of residence referred to in rules 1 and 2 of article 500 shall not be considered as interrupted by obtaining leaves asked for by the interested party or by a voyage or residence in the Peninsula to which the officers are compelled, when by order of the Government they are transferred from the Philippine Islands to those of Cuba and Puerto Rico and *vice versa*.

ART. 506. Authorization of residence of colonial officers after the periods of leaves fixed by the regulations have elapsed is absolutely prohibited.

ART. 507. Leaves for the Peninsula shall not be granted at the same time to two associate justices of the same court in case of a criminal audiencia, or to more than one-third of the associate justices in case of a territorial audiencia, including that of Habana. Leaves, likewise, shall not be taken at the same time by two officers of the department of public prosecution belonging to the same superior court or by the judge and the *promotor* of the same district. Only in the audiencia of Habana may two officers of the department of public prosecution make use of leaves for the Peninsula at the same time.

In granting leaves in the cases referred to above, preference shall be given to the officer who shall have served a longer period without taking a leave.

ART. 508. When officers who have obtained leaves make a direct voyage for the Peninsula or to any other point of Europe, Asia, or America, the day of landing shall be considered as the date on which their leave begins, which they shall prove in a certificate, issued by the captain of a port or by the Spanish consul, according as to whether the point of destination of the voyage is in the Peninsula or outside thereof, respectively.

If the voyage is not direct, the time of the leave shall be counted from the date of embarkation from the colonial province in which the employee resides.

ART. 509. To fulfill the obligations imposed upon an officer on leave he shall conform to the following rules:

1. Employees making use of a leave must have their return embarkation certified to before the time allowed for the leave has expired. This shall be effected by means of a certification of the captain of the port of embarkation from the Peninsula or of the Spanish consul of the place abroad from which they begin their journey.

They shall likewise prove their arrival at the point of their office by a certificate of the captain of the port.

Both certifications shall be made in duplicate. One of these they shall send to the colonial department and the other to the intendant or director of the treasury of the province in which they serve.

2. Any voluntary detention or interruption of the return voyage after having made use of a leave shall cause the forfeiture of the office.

3. Whenever, at the expiration of the time allowed for a leave, the employees to whom said leaves have been granted do not have their

reembarkation for the point at which they hold offices certified, they shall be declared suspended, counting from the date of expiration of the term of the leave.

4. Leaves shall become void which are not made use of within two months after having been communicated to the persons interested if said leaves have been granted for Europe and between Asia and America, and within one month if issued for points on the same or neighboring islands, whether of the Antilles or of the Philippine archipelago.

Those granted to employees obtaining new offices shall likewise become void, without regard as to whether said employees are making use of the same or not.

5. Transportation expenses shall not be paid under any circumstances to employees on leave, no matter what is the cause thereof or to what point the employee on leave may go.

CHAPTER III.

COMMISSIONS.

ART. 510. Commissions for service in the Peninsula shall be conferred only on account of extraordinary and urgent needs of the State, shown in a written communication of the higher authorities of the colonies, if the granting of the same emanates from these authorities, or in a royal order if they are determined by the colonial department.

ART. 511. Said concessions can only be conferred for the period of four months, which can not be extended, counting from the time of landing at a port of the Peninsula after a direct voyage from the place of employment, to the presiding judges and *fiscales* of territorial audiencias, with a right during the entire duration of the commission to the personal pay of the office which they fill regularly and one-half in addition, and to the traveling expenses both ways, duly justified.

ART. 512. Officers coming to the Peninsula from the said provinces in commission of the service shall prove immediately on presenting themselves at the colonial department that they have made a direct voyage. If they should not have done so, they shall lose the right to transportation at the expense of the State and to the emoluments allowed them on account of their extraordinary duties, and shall be obliged to refund to the public treasury the sum advanced to them on either account. In such case they shall be obliged to return to the place of the office which they regularly fill within the period of thirty days, which can not be extended, counted from the date of their landing, during which period they shall have no right to any pay.

ART. 513. Extraordinary commissions for the service may also be conferred in special circumstances for places within the colonial province in which the employee who is given the same fills his office, and if said employee must leave the place of his residence he shall have a right to the pay, extra pay, and in addition one-half of the total pay during the duration of the commission, which can never exceed three months. They shall also be allowed traveling expenses both ways.

ART. 514. In the future no addition of the officers of the colonial possessions to the colonial department or to any other office of the administration of the Peninsula shall be decreed.

ART. 515. Every officer coming to the Peninsula otherwise than under the conditions established in this decree-law, on leave or in commission for the service, even if either has been granted through an error or the negligence of his hierarchical superiors, shall be discharged from the service. The order of discharge shall be retroactive to the day on which said officer ceased to perform the regular duties of his office.

ART. 516. Notwithstanding the provisions of article 514, officers of the judicial and the public prosecution services may be detailed to the codification commission of the colonial provinces for the period of four months at the utmost, which can not be extended. To said details only such officers can be appointed who actually hold the office of associate justice of a territorial audiencia, in the proportion of one officer for each of the same and two officers for that of Habana. The number of officers thus detailed can not exceed three.

ART. 517. The period of four months shall be counted from the date of landing in the Peninsula for the officers who obtain a commission while residing in the colonial provinces at the time when the same is conferred, and from the date of the royal order conferring the commission for those residing in the Peninsula at the time thereof.

ART. 518. The officer who, in any of the cases referred to in this chapter, has not had his embarkation certified to within the period for which the commission is conferred, shall be considered as resigning his office and shall be declared suspended.

ART. 519. The provisions of this title are hereby extended to the officers of the department of public prosecution.

FINAL PROVISION.

All legal provisions conflicting with those of this decree-law are hereby repealed.

Approved by Her Majesty:

FABIÉ.

MADRID, *January 5, 1891.*

APPENDICES.

APPENDICES.

Royal decree of April 3, 1884, declaring the termination of the application of all the temporary provisions of the additional law to the organic law on judicial power.[1]

STATEMENT.

SIR: Few subjects have been the object of such varying laws as the appointment and promotion of the officers of the administration of justice. The noble purpose to give due consideration to legitimate aspirations and interests, together with the great changes in the organization of courts, has produced such a complication of series of succession, categories, assimilations of rank, entrance into the service, and provisional powers that it is very difficult, even with the best intentions, now to proceed in so delicate a matter without offending legitimate hopes, and even rights that should be respected. Nevertheless, it is necessary to devise a remedy for a state of things which has been disturbing, for reasons lying beyond the control of anyone, the personnel of so important a branch of service, unexpected promotions being given to some, others being forced to wait, while, on the other hand, persons have been taken into the service who, according to the laws, could not hope for admission.

Reforms of so radical a type as would conform with the desires of the undersigned secretary can not be proposed by him to Your Majesty at the present time, as he has too much respect for matters which, directly or indirectly, are of a judicial character to interfere with them to any extent without a previous decision of the Parliament; but one painful, though brief, experience has demonstrated to him the imperative necessity of regulating without delay that organism which, more than any other branch of the service, demands order and respect. seniority and hierarchy, modest, but certain, hopes of reward for diligence in work and the removal of personal influence, and which, unfortunately for some time, has been suffering from defects diametrically opposed to such conditions.

The only thing which can for the present be effected, and which is really of the greatest urgency, is to limit arbitrary ministerial decisions, which seldom prove beneficial in countries which, like our own, have a political parliamentary government, united with a social democratic organization, and to secure this it is probably more important, instead of elaborating new substantive precepts, to seek a method of procedure which will insure a vigorous fulfillment of the precepts which have already been promulgated.

It is sad to say it, but in this, as in the other branches of our administrative legistration, the perfection of the written law contrasts with the difficulties of long-sustained and efficacious practice. Thus the

---

[1] All the articles of this decree are still in force except articles 7 and 8, which were repealed by royal decree of April 8, 1886; consequently it must be observed, taking into consideration the provisions of subsequent decisions concerning the various series of succession.

artistic and complicated provisions concerning series of succession of the organic law of 1870, and of the additional law of 1882, satisfy the most exacting spirit by their variety and method; but the provisions on the bureau of personnel seem never to have acquired an actual application, certainly not by the fault of the governments, but for want of regulations to carry these precepts into effect. This consideration awakens in the undersigned secretary a fear that he may not be more successful in the future; but he has been moved by the desire to make the greatest endeavor in seeking additional formulas and guaranties for carrying into effect the law which is in force, and the provisions of which are more ample in what refers to the freedom of ministerial powers in matters of promotions and appointments than the criterion of the present Government would permit, but which would effect a real progress under the sole condition of their being actually carried into effect.

To this end, the provisions of the additional law relating to entrance and promotion being in the essence respected, the undersigned secretary having believed that his right to change by a decree the series of succession established in favor of certain classes is at least doubtful, the temporary provisions, the raison d'être of which has disappeared, shall be without force; a minimum limit of two years is fixed as a prerequisite to promotion from one category to another; the Government renounces the freedom given to it by the law to select for promotion officers of the immediate list, no matter what position said officers may occupy; and the observance of the series of succession is regulated by means of registry books accessible to those interested, open to the public (which is the highest guaranty of modern organizations), whenever such publicity is advisable, for the defense of a right or the denouncement of an abuse or negligence; all guarantied by real competitions for filling the positions of a social importance not lower than that of professors or registers of property, and with administrative and litigative appeals which demand from persons who rashly persist in an error, or in the violation of a right which should be respected, a moderate liability, which for that very reason is apparently true and efficacious.

Much will be left for further work, even after securing by these means the strict fulfillment of the law in force. But it has already been said by one of our statesmen of the seventeenth century "that there is no high aim without much labor," and the undersigned secretary must bear this saying in mind in order not to fall into the error of attractive but ephemeral improvisations; and when the entrance and promotions shall have been regulated in law and in practice, and when the consequences of past modifications shall have vanished, greater and bolder steps may safely be undertaken in the great work of making the judicial organism as vigorous as is demanded by the institutions of a country having parliamentary rule.

At the royal feet of Your Majesty.

FRANCISCO SILVELA.

MADRID, *April 3, 1884.*

ROYAL DECREE.

In conformity with the suggestion of the secretary of grace and justice, with the approval of the council of secretaries, I decree the following:

ART. 1. The application of all the temporary provisions of the additional law to the organic law on judicial power of October 14, 1882, is hereby declared at an end, and therefore the other precepts of the said law remain in force and must be rigorously observed.

ART. 2. A promotion can not be granted to any officer in the judicial service who has not filled for at least two years an office of the class next lower in the respective list.

In default of an officer filling for two years the office in the next lower class in the list, the officer occupying the first place on the graded list shall be promoted.

ART. 3. In the four series of succession fixed in Arts. 41, 42, 43, 44, and 45 of the said additional law, the power which is granted the Government to appoint officers of the class next lower, whatever may be their number on the graded scale, shall be reduced to those who are included in the first two-thirds of their respective grade.

ART. 4. To procure due guaranty and regularity for the series of succession established by the additional law, there shall be kept in the bureau of personnel of audiencias and inferior courts of this department the following books corresponding to the order of promotion established in the said law:

1. For the vacancies of inferior courts of the entrance category.

2. For the vacancies of inferior courts of the promotion category and of the public prosecutors (*abogacias fiscales*) of criminal audiencias.

3. For the vacancies of the inferior courts of the final category, of the public prosecutors (*abogacias fiscales*) of territorial audiencias, and of the *tenientes fiscales* of criminal audiencias.

4. For the vacancies of the associate justices of criminal audiencias, *tenientes fiscales* of territorial audiencias, and *abogados fiscales* of the audiencia of Madrid.

5. For the vacancies of the presiding judges and *fiscales* of criminal audiencias, and of associate justices of territorial audiencias, and of the judges of Madrid.

6. For the vacancies of presiding judges of chambers of territorial audiencias, *fiscales*, associate justices of the territorial audiencia of Madrid, *tenientes fiscales* of the same, or *abogados fiscales* of the supreme court.

7. For the vacancies occurring in the office of associate justices of the supreme court.

ART. 5. In these books, which shall be kept and rubricated by the chief of personnel under the immediate direction of the assistant secretary of this department, there shall be recorded the appointments made in each group of those established by the law, with the observance of the series of succession in the order fixed by the additional law, which shall be counted for vacancies occurring from the date of the publication of this decree in the *Gaceta de Madrid*. These books shall be open to the active and suspended officers of the judicial service who may request to see them at the assistant secretary's office of the department, and said officers shall be given, upon request, certified extracts from these books, at their expense.

ART. 6. The officers who believe themselves to have been prejudiced by an appointment made with an improper modification of the series of succession, may appeal to the secretary through administrative channels. In such an appeal a hearing must be given to the section of grace and justice of the council of state, and legal steps of a litigative character may be brought against the decision of the secretary.

If the litigation shall have demonstrated an improper modification of the series of succession and the illegality of the appointment, the costs of the litigation shall be charged personally to the secretary who may have disregarded the administrative complaint, if the decision of the council of state was not observed.

ART. 7. All the vacancies of the judicial service shall be announced for the purpose of filling them in the *Gaceta de Madrid* as soon as they are officially communicated to the department, and those desiring to be appointed to fill said vacancies shall send within the period of twenty days, counting from the date of the publication of the announcement, their written petitions, accompanied by documents proving their legal eligibility. The bureau of the department shall classify them and shall make a list, making a succinct statement of the proceedings, showing the names of the applicants and their merits, which shall be published with the appointment.

ART. 8. If in any of the series of succession no officers request the promotion due them, that series of succession shall be passed over, a memorandum to that effect being entered in the proper book, and the vacancy being filled from the series of succession next in order.

ART. 9. The duties to be discharged in vacant offices while the steps for filling said offices are in progress may be discharged through a commission for service, which may be intrusted to officers of the same or the next lower category if the circumstances should make it advisable that they should be performed by the person who ordinarily should do so temporarily.

Given at the Palace on April 3, 1884.

ALFONSO.

FRANCISCO SILVELA,
Secretary of Grace and Justice.

(*Gaceta* of April 4.)

Royal order of March 14, 1885, for taking possession of offices, duration and postponement thereof, and transfers of judicial officers.

The attention of this department has been called to the repeated petitions of officers in the judicial and public prosecution service who have taken part in competitions, asking for prolongation of the period fixed by law for taking possession for the purpose of performing their duties and requesting at the same time transfers to positions other than those which must be filled and to which said officers have solicited appointment; as well as to the fact that similar requests of postponement of taking possession are made by many officers who in compliance with their wishes have been transferred without sufficient grounds in either case, except in cases of duly proven sickness that can not be foreseen by said officers before taking part in the competition for appointment or before asking for a transfer. The granting of such postponements, besides necessitating a long temporary filling of vacancies, on account of which the offices remain vacant during the time of competitive examination, as well as during the time of transfer to take possession of the office, causes serious delay in the transaction of business and disturbs the good administration of justice, because the regular incumbents are not performing their duties. The above applies especially to courts of first instance and examination, because frequently the municipal judge who should replace the regular officer in the exercise of his jurisdiction is not a lawyer—a circumstance which again proves to be the cause of a further delay and impediment to the transaction of business. With the object of remedying these evils, removing the inconveniences produced thereby in the ordinary and normal routine of courts, His Majesty the King (whom God preserve) has decreed the following:

1. Officers who in virtue of a competition have been promoted to the vacancies which they desired to fill must take possession of their offices within the period fixed for the purpose in the provisional law on judicial power, which can not be extended, except in case of sickness duly proven. If said period has elapsed, and the officers in question have not taken possession of their offices, it shall be presumed that said officers renounce the promotion, and another officer shall be selected from among those who have applied to fill the same vacancies and have taken part in the same competitive examinations while the former shall remain in the offices they previously held, if their filling has not already been announced, in which latter case they shall be given another office of the same class and category.

2. A promoted officer can not request a transfer until at least one year has elapsed from the date of his promotion, except in cases of incompatibility, when a change of place with another officer should be solicited by means of a petition, or in cases when the officer in question is prevented by serious causes from remaining in the place in which he performs his duties.

3. An extension of the period for taking possession of offices shall not be granted to the officers who have been transferred at their own request, except in cases of sickness duly proven, a statement concerning which must appear in the petition. Said petition shall be directed through the proper channels, and therein the petitioner shall comply with the other requirements which for petitious for leaves and their extensions are fixed by the royal order of July 24, 1878, issued by the treasury department for carrying into effect the provisions of article 43 of the budget law of said year.

4. Every request for transfer shall be made in the form of a petition directed through the respective presiding judges of territorial audiencias, in which there shall be stated the reasons for the request, for which purpose there shall be kept in this department a registry in which a memorandum of said petitions shall be made.

I communicate this to you for your information and that of the officers of that judicial territory, and for other purposes in connection therewith.

May God preserve you many years.

SILVELA.

MADRID, *March 14, 1885.*
To the Presiding Judge and the Fiscal of the Audiencia of ———.
(*Gaceta* of March 18.)

———

Law of August 19, 1885, on the unification of the judicial and the public prosecution services of the Peninsula and the colonies.

Don Alfonso XII, by the grace of God, constitutional King of Spain. To all who shall hear or see these presents:

Be it known that the Cortes have decreed and we have sanctioned the following:

ART. 1. The judicial and public prosecution services of the Peninsula and the colonies are hereby united, and equal rights are granted to the officers of the same within their respective categories, subject to the laws in force in so far as they are not modified by the present one.

ART. 2. For the fulfillment of the provisions of the preceding article the following grades are established in the judicial service:

1. The presiding judge of the supreme court.
2. The presiding judges of the chambers of the same.
3. The associate justices of same court.
4. The presiding judge and the presiding judges of chambers of the audiencias of Madrid and Habana.
5. The associate justices of the audiencias of Madrid and Habana and the presiding judge and the presiding judges of chambers of territorial audiencias.
6. The associate justices of territorial audiencias, presiding judges of criminal audiencias, and the judges of first instance of Madrid and Habana.
7. The associate justices of criminal audiencias.
8. The judges of first instance of the final category.
9. The judges of the promotion category.
10. The judges of the entrance category.

ART. 3. The hierarchical order of the department of public prosecution shall be as follows:

1. The *fiscal* of the supreme court.
2. The *teniente fiscal* of the same and the *fiscales* of the audiencias of Madrid and Habana.
3. The *abogados fiscales* of the supreme court, the *tenientes fiscales* of the audiencias of Madrid and Habana, and the *fiscales* of territorial audiencias.
4. The *fiscales* of criminal audiencias.
5. The *tenientes fiscales* of territorial audiencias and the *abogados fiscales* of the audiencias of Madrid and Habana.
6. The *abogados fiscales* of territorial audiencias, the *tenientes fiscales* of criminal audiencias, and the *promotores fiscales* of the audiencia of Habana.
7. The *abogados fiscales* of criminal audiencias and the *promotores* of the final category serving in the colonies.
8. The *promotores* of the promotion category serving in the colonies.
9. The *promotores* of the entrance category serving in the colonies.

ART. 4. The first grade in the public prosecution service is equivalent to the second grade in the judicial service; the second of the former to the fourth of the latter; the third of the former to the fifth of the latter; the fourth of the former to the sixth of the latter, and to that of the secretary of the supreme court; the fifth of the public prosecution to the seventh of the judicial; the sixth to the eighth, and to that of the secretaries of chamber and of administration of the audiencias of Madrid and Habana; the seventh of the former to the ninth of the latter and to that of secretaries of chamber and of administration of the territorial audiencia; the eighth to the tenth of the judicial service and to that of the secretaries of territorial audiencias, and the ninth to that of vice-secretaries.

ART. 5. The department of grace and justice shall arrange the general graded list within the period of three months, counting from the date of the promulgation of this law, in which there shall be included all the officers of the judicial service and of the department of public prosecution of the whole kingdom, in conformity with the provisions of the royal decree of September 27, 1878.

The department of the colonies shall forward to the department of grace and justice the necessary data in order that there may be included in the graded list the officers of the said services who fill offices or are on the list of suspended officers of America and Asia. It shall likewise forward also within the first fifteen days of each year a statement of the changes occurring in the partial graded list which said department must make in its turn in order to make the proper corrections in the general one.

ART. 6. Entrance into the judicial service in the Peninsula shall take place as judge of the entrance category by means of a competitive examination, in conformity with the provisions of article 35 of the additional law to the provisional law or organization of the judicial power, and without prejudice to the power granted to the Government to name a fourth series of succession for those possessing the qualifications required by article 40 of the law above mentioned.

Until the present organization in the colonies is modified entrance into the service shall take place as *promotor* of the entrance category, the appointee being required to possess the qualifications prescribed in article 19 of the royal decree of September 20, 1875, excepting the power which in the provision in question and in the additional law is reserved to the Government. To the colonies there shall be extended the articles of the above-mentioned law that establish the series of succession for filling vacancies, including therein *promotores* and other judicial officers in their proper places according to the classification of article 4 of this law.

ART. 7. The secretaries of grace and justice and the colonial secretary, in conformity with the said series of succession and taking into account the organization of the superior courts of their respective departments, shall fill the vacancies that occur with officers dependent on said departments, and may appoint in the third and fourth series the officers who request transfer or promotion from one to the other. In order to aspire to the former the officers of the colonial department must have served four years in the colonies, or in the direction of grace and justice of the colonial department, and two years in the category. This last condition is required also of those serving in the Peninsula who request a transfer to the said provinces. For a promotion the officers of either department must possess the qualifications required by the law cited. Should duly qualified candidates be wanting, or should they not possess the qualifications required by law, appointments shall be made from among the officers selected from said series.

ART. 8. The places referred to in article 46 of the said additional law and included in the respective grades of articles 2 and 3 of the present law shall be filled in the manner prescribed by the former, one of each three vacancies occurring in the Peninsula or in the colonies being given to officers of the colonies or of the peninsula belonging to the classes specified in said articles, who must have served for two years in their category and must request the appointment.

ART. 9. The secretaries referred to above shall take into consideration, in filling the position referred to in articles 46, 47, and 48 of the said additional law, the seniority granted in the general graded list to the officers eligible for the positions in question, and the merits that commend them for the vacancies occurring in their respective departments.

ART. 10. For the purposes of article 50 of the additional law the associate justice of the greatest seniority of the audiencia of Habana is hereby granted the same privileges as are given by said article to the associate justice of the greatest seniority of the audiencia of Madrid.

ART. 11. In filling offices of secretaries of chamber and administration of the final category of the territorial audiencias of the Kingdom, and the offices of the secretary and the vice secretary of the supreme court, articles 54 and 55 of the said additional law shall be observed.

ART. 12. For the transfer or promotion of the officers referred to in this law from the Peninsula to the colonies, or *rice versa*, a request must be made by the officers themselves. Those of the colonies must also have to their credit four years of residence in said colonies and two years of service in the category, unless the appointment conforms with the succession by seniority.

The petitions shall be addressed to the secretary making the appointment, through the department in which the petitioner serves, who in passing upon the petition shall add a report of the career and memoranda concerning the officer in question and his record of service. The latter shall be published in the *Gaceta de Madrid*, together with the appointment, with a citation of the article of the law on which it is based.

ART. 13. The categories and privileges acquired in conformity with the provisions and laws in force granted to those holding the same shall be respected.

The officers who entered the service in the colonies without a competitive examination, subsequently to the date of the promulgation of the organic law on judicial power, shall be required to serve the time of service equivalent to that which the additional law on law practice fixes for lawyers for entering the respective category, before they can be transferred to the Peninsula, and two years more before they can be promoted.

ART. 14. The officers who are lawyers of the department of grace and justice, and those of the direction of grace and justice of the colonial department, shall preserve the category and position in the graded list that may have been granted them, when they have completed the length of service required to this effect of the officers of the same rank in the judicial and the public prosecution services. Those who hereafter enter either service can not aspire to the categories, and consequently can not be included in the graded list if they do not belong to the same, in which case their categories shall not be accepted as superior to that which they had and with which they entered the department. Those who shall hereafter enter the service in the direction of grace and justice in the same manner as the officers of that department can not be promoted without having completed the necessary time of service required for promotion in their respective category.

ART. 15. The provisions on incompatibility prescribed for judicial officers by article 111 of the organic law on judicial power shall be rigorously enforced in the colonies. From this provision shall be excepted, as long as the present organization in the Philippines is preserved, the judges of the Philippines who by virtue of their duties discharge other functions besides those of the judicial office, in conformity with the laws in force in said provinces.

The secretary of grace and justice and the secretary of the colonies shall see to the fulfillment of this law.

Therefore:

We command all superior courts, judges, chiefs, governors, and all other authorities, civil as well as military and ecclesiastical, of whatsoever class and rank, to observe and cause to be observed, fulfill and execute the present law in all its parts.

Given at San Ildefonso on August 19, 1885.

I, THE KING.

ANTONIO CÁNOVAS DEL CASTILLO,
    President of the Council of Secretaries.

(*Gaceta*, August 22.)

123

Royal decree of September 9, 1885, issued for the compliance of the law of August 19 of the same year, unifying the judicial and the public prosecution services of the Peninsula and of the colonies.

For the due fulfillment of the provisions of the law on unification of the judicial and the public prosecution services of the colonies and of the Peninsula, dated August 19 of the current year, in matters referring to the department of the colonies, on the recommendation of the secretary of this branch of service, and in accord with the secretary of grace and justice, I decree the following:

ARTICLE 1. The series of appointments concerning inferior courts of the promotion category and other higher categories, which were established by my royal decree of the 29th of last May, shall be considered as substituted by those established by the law of October 14, 1882, additional to the organic law on judicial power, according to the provisions of article 6 of said law on unification, and by the provisions of the latter included in articles 7 and 8. In all other matters which do not oppose said law the said royal decree mentioned above shall remain in force.

ART. 2. The colonial department shall forward to the department of grace and justice the graded list of the personnel of its department, with the necessary notes, remarks, and facts which serve as proof, which should be necessary within the period of thirty days counted from the date of the promulgation of the law on unification above mentioned, in order to comply with the provisions of article 5 of the same, and said department shall likewise forward in the month of January of each year a statement of the changes which took place in the previous year. In either case the officers of the direction of grace and justice of the colonial department, who are lawyers, referred to in article 14 of the said law, shall be included in the category granted to them, with the proper notices concerning the length of service with which the officers referred to and the officers of the secretary's office of the department of grace and justice have to reach the seniority required for said categories.

ART. 3. In the single graded list and in its annual renewals a statement shall be made that said graded list has been drafted with the approval of the colonial secretary.

ART. 4. Claims made by officers of the colonial branch against the classification of their rights or category which appears in the graded list, shall be decided upon by the secretaries of grace and justice and of the colonies conjointly. Should there be a disagreement between the departments the decision shall be submitted to the council of secretaries.

ART. 5. The provisions of the present decree referring to the appointment of officers shall be in force from the date of the publication of the general graded list of the unified services in the *Gaceta de Madrid*. In the meanwhile the royal decree of April 12, 1875, and of May 29 of the current year shall be strictly observed in reference to filling offices.

ART. 6. Officers of the colonies and of the Peninsula, both active and suspended, and other persons who are eligible to the vacancies that occur, must request their appointment to said vacancies officially, according to the provisions of the last of the above-mentioned decrees.

Given at the Palace on September 9, 1885.

ALFONSO.

MANUEL AGUIRRE DE TEJADA,
Secretary of the Colonies.

(*Gaceta*, September 11.)

Royal decree of April 8, 1886, on the manner of filling vacancies in the judicial and the public prosecution services.

In conformity with the recommendation of the secretary of grace and justice, with the approval of the council of secretaries, I decree the following:

ART. 1. Article 7 of the royal decree of April 3, 1884, is hereby repealed.

Vacancies in the judical and public prosecution services shall be filled by the Government without a previous announcement in the *Gaceta*, in accordance with the provisions of the additional law to the law on judicial power of October 14, 1882, and other prescriptions of the royal decree above referred to.

ART. 2. In every appointment made in conformity with the provision of the preceding article there shall be stated the series of succession to which the filling of said vacancy corresponds, and the number occupied by the promoted officer in the graded list.

Said appointment shall be published in the *Gaceta* with the record of merits and services of the appointee.

ART. 3. All other provisions of the royal decree of April 3, 1884, shall remain in force.

Given at the Palace on April 8, 1886.

MARÍA CRISTINA.

MANUEL ALFONSO MARTINEZ,
Secretary of Grace and Justice.

(*Gaceta*, April 10.)

Royal decree of December 26, 1886, issued in compliance with article 5 of the law of August 19, 1885.

In view of the reasons given by the president of the council of secretaries, with the approval of the said council and of the section of state and grace and justice of the council of state, I decree the following:

ART. 1. The officers of the administration of justice in the colonial possessions shall appear in the general graded list provided for in article 5 of the law on unification of the judicial and the public prosecution services, with the seniority resulting from the date on which they took possession of their offices.

ART. 2. In conformity with article 50 of the additional law to the organic law on judicial power, the right of the associate justice of the greatest seniority of the audiencia of Madrid for promotion to the supreme court belongs solely to the officer who has actually served in said audiencia for the greatest number of years.

ART. 3. The officers assimilated to the judicial and the public prosecution services can not be included in the graded list until they possess the conditions required to obtain the corresponding category.

ART. 4. As a consequence of the provisions of the preceding article assimilated officers can not assume greater seniority than that resulting from the date on which said officers comply with the conditions required for the office that has been assimilated.

ART. 5. The officers included in articles 3 and 4 must prove to the department of grace and justice that they possess the qualifications required by the orders granting the assimilation in order that, after the proper declaration, they may be included in the general graded list, in accordance with the provisions of article 4.

Given at the Palace on December 26, 1886.

MARÍA CRISTINA.

PRÁXEDES MATEO SAGASTA,
President of the Council of Secretaries.

(*Gaceta*, December 28.)

Royal decree of February 25, 1887, recognizing the codification commission of the colonial provinces.

In view of the reasons given to me by the secretary of the colonies, I decree the following:

ART. 1. The codification commission of the colonies is hereby reorganized as follows: The number of members shall be 14, the director-general of grace and justice of the colonial department being one of them.

ART. 2. The members of the commission must be lawyers residing in Madrid and of acknowledged competency in judicial matters, a part of the members should be selected from among persons of recognized knowledge in the different branches of colonial legislation.

ART. 3. The secretary of the colonies may add temporarily to the commission a number of associate justices of the audiencias of Cuba, Puerto Rico, or the Philippines, according to the demands of work with which said commission is occupied and subject to the provisions of article 13 of the royal decree of the 3d of last December.

ART. 4. The Government shall appoint a president, a vice-president, and a secretary of the commission from among its members.

ART. 5. These offices, as well as that of the other members of the commission, shall be honorary and without pay.

ART. 6. The codification commission shall have the obligation to study and draft the projects of codes for observance in the colonies, to report whenever ordered by the secretary on the interpretation and incidents of the application of said codes, and to propose or indicate any points of the common colonial legislation which, in their judgment, it would be proper to reform.

ART. 7. For transacting the business of the secretary's office and other work of the commission there shall be four auxiliary officers, appointed by the secretary of the colonies. The first officer shall draw a salary of 3,000 pesetas; the second 2,500 pesetas; the third 2,000 pesetas, and the fourth 1,500 pesetas. The first three must be lawyers.

ART. 8. The salaries of said officers shall be charged to the appropriation for the expenses of the codification commission of the colonies in the respective budgets of the colonial provinces, the necessary amount of the appropriation for material of the commission being transferred to the sum allowed for the personnel of the same.

ART. 9. The provisions that conflict with those of the present decree are hereby repealed.

Given at the Palace on February 25, 1887.

MARÍA CRISTINA.

VICTOR BALAGUER,
Secretary of the Colonies.

Royal decree of August 12, 1887, extending to the Spanish colonial provinces and possessions the provisional law of June 18, 1870, establishing rules for the exercise of pardon.

STATEMENT.

MADAM: The exercise of pardon, which in all the times has been considered as one of the most beautiful privileges of the Crown, is applied in our colonial provinces without being subject to fixed rules and with such obstacles and inconveniences in its exercise that many a time complaints can not reach the throne from those who, rather more unfortunate than guilty, have committed a crime, or who, repenting their former life, desire to return to the society which has expelled them, and to become its useful and beneficial members.

In order to avoid these evils, and being anxious to introduce among this large part of the Spanish nationality all laws tending to improve the administration of the same, the Government of Your Majesty desires to extend to Cuba, Puerto Rico, and the Philippines, by means of a Royal decree, the law of June 18, 1870, which regulates the granting of pardons in the Peninsula, with such modifications which it has deemed advisable to introduce in conformity with the report of the council of state and the codification commission of the colonies. The Government entertains the conviction that Your Majesty, who manifests such zeal and predilection in the present and the future of those distant colonies, will deign to sign in the name of Your Majesty's august son this legal measure which introduces in the same and in their administration of justice so important an improvement.

In view of these reasons the undersigned secretary has the honor to submit to the approval of Your Majesty the accompanying project of a decree.

At the Royal feet of Your Majesty,

VICTOR BALAGUER.

SAN ILDEFONSO, *August 12, 1887.*

ROYAL DECREE.

In view of the reasons given by the secretary of the colonies, and with the approval of the council of secretaries, in the name of my august son the King, Don Alfonso XIII, and as Queen Regent of the Realm, I decree the following:

To the islands of Cuba, Puerto Rico, the Philippines, and the other Spanish colonial possessions there is hereby extended the provisional law of June 10, 1870, in force in the Peninsula for the exercise of pardons, with the modifications of the articles specified below, and which have been introduced in conformity with the opinion of the council of state and of the codification commission for the colonies.

This law shall become operative as soon as its promulgation is announced in the gacetas of the respective islands.

Given at San Ildefonso on August 12, 1887.

MÁRIA CRISTINA.

VICTOR BALAGUER, *Secretary of the Colonies.*

Provisional law of July 18, 1870, establishing rules for the exercise of pardon, with the suitable modifications for its application to the colonial provinces.

CHAPTER I.

PERSONS WHO MAY BE PARDONED.

ART. 1. Criminals guilty of any kind of crimes may be pardoned in conformity with the provisions of this law, and absolved from the whole or part of the punishment incurred by said crimes.

ART. 2. From the provisions of the preceding article are excepted—

1. Defendants in criminal trials upon whom a final sentence has not yet been pronounced.

2. Those who have not been at the disposal of the court pronouncing the sentence for the execution of the penalty imposed.

3. Second offenders in the same or in any other crime, for which they have been condemned by a final sentence. Nevertheless, an exception shall be made in the cases in which, in the judgment of the court pronouncing the sentence, or of the council of state, there are sufficient reasons of justice, equity, or public convenience for granting the pardon.

ART. 3. The provisions of the preceding article shall not be applicable to criminals condemned for the crimes included in Chapters 1 and 2, Title 2, Book 2, and Chapters 1, 2, and 3, of the same book of the Penal Code.

CHAPTER II.

THE KINDS OF PARDONS AND THEIR EFFECTS.

ART. 4. Pardons may be either full or partial. A full pardon shall be an absolution from all penalties to which the criminal may have been sentenced, and which he has not yet executed.

A partial pardon shall consist of an absolution from one or more of the penalties imposed, or from a part of all the penalties incurred which have not yet been executed by the criminal.

A commutation of the sentence or sentences imposed upon the criminal to milder sentences shall also be considered as a partial pardon.

ART. 5. A grant of pardon, in which at least the principal penalty which is the object of the pardon is not specifically mentioned, shall be considered null and of no effect, nor shall it be executed by the proper court.

ART. 6. A pardon absolving from the principal penalty shall include also an absolution from the accessory penalties imposed upon the criminal with the former, with the exception of the penalty of disqualification for public offices, and for political privileges, and of subjection to the surveillance of authorities, which shall not be considered as included, unless a special mention to that effect is made in its grant.

Civil indemnifications shall likewise never be included in pardons.

ART. 7. A pardon may be granted for accessory penalties, with the exclusion of the principal ones, and *vice versa*, unless they are indispensable by their nature and effects.

ART. 8. A pardon absolving from a pecuniary fine shall exempt the person pardoned from paying the sum not yet paid by him; but said pardon shall not include the refunding of the part already paid, unless a decision to this effect is expressly made.

ART. 9. A pardon can not be granted to exempt from the payment of judicial costs and expenses of the trial which are not due to the

State; but a pardon may be granted for a subsidiary fine which an insolvent who has been fined would in this connection have to suffer.

ART. 10. If a person fined has died at the time or after the time when sufficient causes exist for granting a pardon, the heirs of that person may be freed from the accessory fine of the penalty, in conformity with the provisions of articles 8 and 9.

ART. 11. A full pardon shall be granted to the persons fined only in the case when, in the opinion of the court pronouncing the sentence and of the council of state, there exist in his favor reasons of justice, equity, or public convenience.

In all other cases only a partial pardon shall be granted, and preferably a commutation of the sentence imposed to another sentence of less gravity within the same graduated scale.

Notwithstanding the provisions of the preceding paragraph, a sentence may also be commuted to another imposing a penalty within another different scale whenever there are sufficient grounds for such action in the opinion of the court pronouncing the sentence, or of the council of state, and, moreover, when the condemned agrees with the commutation.

ART. 12. When the principal sentence has been commuted the accessory sentences shall also be considered commuted to the other ones which, according to the provisions of the code, correspond to the sentence which the person pardoned should have to suffer.

Exceptions shall, however, be made in the case in which pardons are granted with an express order to the contrary.

ART. 13. The commutation of a sentence shall be void from the day on which the person pardoned fails to fulfill, for any reason depending on his will, the penalty which has been imposed on him in the commutation.

ART. 14. The following shall be the implied conditions of every pardon:

1. That no prejudice be caused a third person and no damage be done to their rights.

2. That the condemned person, before obtaining the pardon, must be pardoned by the person offended, if the crime for which he has been sentenced can be prosecuted only at the instance of a party.

ART. 15. In granting pardons there may, moreover, be imposed on the person pardoned all the other conditions suggested by considerations of justice, equity, or public utility.

ART. 16. The court pronouncing the sentence shall not fulfill any pardon the conditions of which have not been previously complied with by the person sentenced, excepting such as could not have been fulfilled on account of their special nature.

ART. 17. The grant of pardon is by its nature irrevocable, subject to the clauses with which it has been conceded.

CHAPTER III.

PROCEDURE OF REQUESTING AND GRANTING PARDONS.

ART. 18. Pardons may be solicited by the persons sentenced, their relatives, or any other person in their behalf without requiring a written power granting them right of representation.

Nevertheless, collective petitions or petitions containing a number of signatures asking pardon in the cause of another party shall not be admitted.

Those of official classes or corporations and of public officers are also prohibited, as provided for in the royal decree of July 1, 1867, extended to the colonies by the royal order of August 13 of the same year.

ART. 19. A grant of pardon may be recommended also by the court pronouncing the sentence, by the supreme court, or by the *fiscal* of either of said courts, in conformity with the provisions of the second paragraph, article 2, of the penal code, and also with the other provisions in the laws on procedure and criminal cassation.

The recommendation shall be confidential until the secretary of the colonies, after examining it, shall order the institution of the proper proceedings.

ART. 20. The Government may also institute the proper proceedings in conformity with the provisions of this law for granting pardons which have not been requested by individuals or recommended by courts of justice.

ART. 21. The petitions for pardons shall be directed to the colonial department through the audiencias and the governors-general.

In case the person sentenced serves the sentence in the penitentiaries of the peninsula or in those of our penal colonies in Africa, the chief of the establishment shall transmit the petition to the secretary of the colonies.

ART. 22. Every petition for pardon shall be accompanied by a confidential report of the chief of the establishment in which the prisoner serves his term concerning the conduct of the condemned, or by a report from the governor of the province in which the person sentenced resides, if the penalty does not deprive the person in question of liberty of action.

The governor of the province, or the chief of the penal establishment, or a diplomatic or consular agent, respectively, must furnish within the period of fifteen days the confidential report referred to in this article. to the person sentenced, who requests it for the purposes of the pardon,

ART. 23. The petitions for pardons, including those presented directly to the colonial department, shall be forwarded to the court which pronounced the sentence, for report, unless such reports have already been added, and said court shall give a hearing to the *fiscal*, or to the party offended, if there be any.

ART. 24. The court which has pronounced the sentence, after hearing the *fiscal* and the offended party, if there be any, shall make a report, stating therein, if possible, the age, status (whether married or single), and occupation of the person sentenced; his wealth, if known; his merits and antecedents; whether he has formerly been prosecuted and condemned for another crime, and whether he served the sentence or was pardoned; for what cause and in what form; the aggravating or extenuating circumstances involved in the perpetration of the crime; the time of preventive imprisonment which he underwent during the prosecution; the part of the sentence that he has served; his conduct after the final sentence, and especially the proofs or indications of repentance that have been observed; whether there are or not any parties offended, and whether the crime causes injury to a third party, and other information that may prove of value in the elucidation of the facts, concluding with the opinion of the court relative to the justice or advisability and form of the pardon to be granted.

This report must be issued by the court which pronounced the sentence within a period not exceeding thirty days, counting from the date on which it received the order to prepare the same.

3007——9

ART. 25. The court which pronounced the sentence shall forward to the colonial department with its report the historical penal record and a certified copy of the final sentence of the condemned, with all the other documents that are deemed necessary for the proof of the facts.

ART. 26. The supreme court and the court which pronounced the sentence, in recommending officially to the Government the granting of pardons, shall at the same time forward with the recommendation the report and the documents referred to in the foregoing articles.

ART. 27. The secretary of the colonies shall thereupon forward the proceedings to the council of state, in order that the colonial section of the same should give in its turn its opinion relative to the justice, equity, or advisability of granting the pardon.

ART. 28. Notwithstanding the provisions of the foregoing articles, a commutation of a death sentence and those imposed for the crimes included in Chapters I and II, Title 2, Book 2, and Chapters I, II, III, Title 3, Book 2 of the Penal Code, may be granted without previously hearing the court which has pronounced the sentence nor the council of state.

ART. 29. A grant of pardon shall be made by means of a decree containing a statement of reasons and approved by the council of secretaries, which shall be published in the *Gaceta de Madrid* and in those of Habana, Puerto Rico, or Manila, as the case may be.

The revocation of the clause of detention shall be granted by a royal order stating the reasons therefor, while the effects of this penalty are in force in the colonial territories.

ART. 30. The execution of a pardon shall be intrusted invariably to the court which pronounced the sentence.

As far as the provisions in force on cassation of criminal matters permit, the governors-general shall preserve the powers granted them by the royal order of May 29, 1855, and those following, and the organic royal decree of June 9, 1878.

ART. 31. A petition or a recommendation for a pardon shall not suspend the execution of a final sentence, except in the case when death sentence has been imposed, which shall not be executed until the Government shall have acknowledged to the court which has pronounced the sentence the receipt of the petition or recommendation.

Royal decree of October 26, 1888, establishing the statistical service of the administration of justice in civil and criminal matters for the islands of Cuba, Puerto Rico, and the Philippines.

In conformity with the recommendation of the secretary of the colonies, with the approval of the council of secretaries; in the name of my august son, the King Don Alfonso XIII, and as Queen Regent of the Realm, I decree the following:

ART. 1. The statistical service of the administration of justice in civil and criminal matters is hereby established for the islands of Cuba, Puerto Rico, and the Philippines, and for this purpose the corresponding bureau is created in the general direction of grace and justice of the colonial department.

ART. 2. The statistics of the administration of justice in criminal matters shall include in separate sections the following groups:

First. A classification of crimes and misdemeanors according to the order, denomination, and method of the penal code, stating the number of crimes, that of the criminals prosecuted, acquitted, or condemned as authors, accomplices, or concealers; punitive, correctional, or light penalties, and cases of imposition of fines, bonds, degradation, civil interdiction, confiscation of the products and instruments of a crime, and costs.

Second. The crimes and misdemeanors which have given rise to proceedings in the territory of each criminal audiencia, classified in the order, denomination, and merit of Titles 1 to 14 of Book 2, and from 1 to 4 of Book 3 of the Penal Code, with a specification of the number of crimes, of the persons tried criminally, acquitted, or condemned to punitive, correctional, and light penalties.

Third. The proceedings carried on in the territory of an audiencia: Oral trials, proceedings brought against senators and deputies, preliminary trials demanding liability, cases in *flagrante delicto*, proceedings for libel and slander against private persons; by printing, drawing, or any other mechanical means of publication, extraditions and proceedings against absent criminals; appeals in cassation for infraction of law or of form, with a specification of those prepared, and those entered, admitted, and refused; complaints to superior authorities for refusal to admit testimony in order to enter an appeal of cassation and appeals for revision; trials of misdemeanor in first and second instance.

Fourth. Classification of criminals according to sex, age, status (whether married or single), description, birthplace, education, profession, or occupation.

Fifth. Classification of repeated offenses, with specification whether they have been repeated once or more, and a subdivision, according to sex, status (whether married or single), description, birthplace, education, and occupation of criminals.

Sixth. Relation between the crimes and individual conditions of criminals, with a specification in each class of crimes, in the order used in the code, of the number of criminals according to sex, age, status (whether married or single), description, birthplace, education, profession, or occupation, and the character of the prosecution.

Seventh. Relation between the territory of criminal audiencias and the individual conditions of criminals according to sex, age, status (whether married or single), description and birthplace, education, profession, or occupation, and the character of the prosecution.

Eighth. Special statistics of oral trials, with the specification of the number of prosecutions, causes finally decided by said procedure, time consumed for their hearing by periods of three months, one year, and more than one year, consent of the criminal, suspension of proceedings, acquittals and condemnatory sentences, causes filed on account of refusal to attend, insane criminals who have become such after the perpetration of the crime, liberty under bail, and provisional imprisonment, with the specification of its duration by quarterly periods; witnesses examined, their number, amount of indemnifications, physicians and specialists taking part, and their fees.

Ninth. Suicides, their number and known or probable causes.

Tenth. General and special pardons, commutations and reduction of penalties, with the specification of the class of crimes to which they refer; changes in the register of condemned persons.

ART. 3. The statistics of the administration of justice in civil matters must include the following groups, elaborated in as many tables as are deemed indispensable for their better understanding:

First. Municipal courts: Instruments of conciliation, classification according to their object and decisions; oral trials classified according to their object, duration, termination, and costs according to the schedule of fees; trials of ejectment, classified by their causes, duration, termination, and costs according to the schedules of fees.

Second. Courts of first instance: Population, superficial area, and a general table of judicial business in civil and commercial matters of each of said courts during the year; appeals taken to courts of first instance from decisions pronounced by municipal courts, and classification of the same, according to whether these sentences have been confirmed or modified wholly or partially; classification by matters of the civil substantive law of affairs decided by the courts of first instance; classification of said business by titles and chapters of the law on civil procedure, their duration, and the amount of costs according to the schedule of fees; commercial matters resolved upon by inferior courts and classified according to the commercial code.

Third. Territorial audiencias: Population, superficial area, and organization of the personnel of each audiencia; a general table of the judicial work of each one of the latter in civil and commercial matters during the year; appeals classified according to the courts of first instance pronouncing the sentences appealed from, and classification of the same according to whether they have been confirmed or modified wholly or partially; classification by matters of the substantive civil law of the business decided upon by the audiencias; classification of the same by titles and chapters of the law on civil procedure, their duration, and costs according to the schedule of fees, commercial matters resolved upon by audiencias, and classified according to the commercial code.

Fourth. The supreme court: Business coming from Cuba, Puerto Rico, and the Philippines; general statement of the civil and commercial matters in which it has had cognizance during the year; appeals in cassation classified according to the matters of the substantive civil law, by titles and chapters of the law on civil procedure and of the commercial code; classification of appeals acording to their termination, and the audiencias pronouncing the judgments that have been appealed from.

Fifth. Voluntary jurisdiction: Decisions of this jurisdiction classified according to their object, their termination, duration, and the amount of costs according to the schedule of fees.

ART. 4. The secretary of the colonies shall circulate the statistical papers, forms, and instructions in order to organize the transmission and the publication of the data.

ART. 5. In order to facilitate the routine of the numerous details occasioned by the organization of this service, the chief of the bureau created with this object in the general direction of grace and justice of the colonial department shall correspond directly with the secretaries of audiencias and chambers, reporting on the matter to the director of this branch.

ART. 6. In the first fifteen days of February of each year the bureau shall publish a statement of those audiencias or chambers which have sent complete statistical data, and suitable proceedings shall be instituted to adopt the proper decision with respect to those which have not forwarded the same.

ART. 7. The secretary of the colonies may order visits of inspection, delegating for the purpose persons of recognized competence and capacity, in order to verify or complete the statistical data, whenever he deems such action necessary.

ART. 8. The bureau of statistics shall be organized with the necessary personnel, the present personnel being utilized whenever possible and increased if it be insufficient, for which purpose the Government shall be granted sufficient funds in harmony with the provisions of the budget laws in force.

Given at the Palace on October 26, 1888.

MÁRIA CRISTINA.

TRINITARIO RUIZ Y CAPDEPON,
Secretary of the Colonies.

Royal order of March 12, 1889, on filling vacancies of the fourth series of succession in the judicial and public prosecution services.

YOUR EXCELLENCY: From the fact that the legislation in force grants to the Government of His Majesty the power to fill vacancies in the fourth series of succession of courts of first instance with lawyers possessing certain qualifications proving their ability and experience in court, there was recognized an excellent principle, the combination of which with scientific culture demonstrated in public debates constitutes the most perfect method for entrance into the judicial service.

It must be admitted that, although said principle in exceptional and distinguished cases has produced excellent results, it has served very often as a mere pretext for the basis of favoritism.

The Cortes of the Kingdom in its high wisdom is called upon to solve definitely the burning problem of recruiting officers from said personnel, taking into consideration the lessons of experience, and above all the necessity of providing a proper reward for certain duties of substitutes, creditably performed, but while the Parliament is making its decision, and especially while there are candidates and officers who have proved their skill in the noble competition of examinations, the vacancies that occur should be awarded them with no other exception or preference than that determined by the strict order of their seniority. In virtue of these considerations Her Majesty (whom God preserve), the Queen Regent of the Realm, in the name of her august son, Don Alfonso XIII, decrees the following:

1. That all vacancies in the courts of the entrance category that shall hereafter occur be filled, in the strict numerical order, with candidates to the judicial service according to the corresponding graded list, and when this list has been exhausted, in the order of seniority with secretaries and vice-secretaries who request them and who hold their offices as regular incumbents, preference being given to those who entered the service through competitive examination.

2. Vacancies in the fourth series of succession that may occur in the graded list of judges of the promotion and final categories shall be filled with secretaries who shall have entered the service in a similar way, and who, besides, possess the qualifications required for promotion by the legislation in force.

To these rules, which I communicate to your excellency by royal order, your excellency will kindly conform in the recommendations for filling vacancies in the ranks of judges of the entrance, promotion, and final categories.

May God preserve Your Excellency many years.

MADRID, *March 12, 1889.*

CANALEJAS Y MÉNDEZ.

To the Assistant Secretary of this Department.
(*Gaceta* of March 13.)

Royal order of March 16, 1889, on promotions in the third series of succession in the judicial and public prosecution services.

YOUR EXCELLENCY: In establishing in the organic law on judicial power and in the additional law to the same a mixed system of promotions, permitting the reward of both the prolonged services and the extraordinary merits earned in the judicial and the public prosecution services, the prerogative of seniority was granted to officers occupying the first places in the graded list of their category.

This system of promotions necessitated a great conservatism in exercising the great powers granted the Government by the series of succession in promotions by merit; but it must be confessed that the promotions have not corresponded to the high motives inspiring the legislator, and have been limited simply to respecting the text of legal provisions. Cases arise, as frequent as painful, when through a series of postponements seldom justifiable, very deserving and zealous officers, to whom fate has been unfavorable, appear in low-grade offices of the graded list of a certain category, and when each promotion follows only after a long period of life spent in the service, until the promotion can not be refused because of seniority.

A bill reforming the organic law has been submitted to the Chambers, and the latter have been intrusted with the establishment of reasonable guaranties for the proper exercise of the appointment power; but meanwhile this department may take notice of legitimate claims and utilize the third series of succession established by the laws in force, in order to compensate for the consequences of unjustifiable postponements, preserving with the second and the fourth a sphere of action which is sufficient and perhaps excessive, giving room to the discretionary judgment of the secretaries.

In virtue of these special considerations, Her Majesty (whom God preserve), the Queen Regent of the Realm, in the name of her august son, the King, Don Alfonso XIII, has decreed the following:

1. That in the future Your Excellency will please recommend for filling vacancies corresponding to the third series of succession that may occur in the graded list of all the categories of the judicial and public prosecution services, except those of associate justices of the supreme court, with officers of the immediately inferior class who possess the qualifications required for promotion by the legislation in force and have to their credit the greatest number of years in the service.

2. That for the fulfillment of this sovereign provision a special graded list be made and published, in which the officers of each category, without discrimination between the judicial and public prosecution services, shall be arranged in strict order of seniority, computed for the actual time spent in the said service.

I communicate the above by royal order to your excellency for your excellency's information and consequent effect.

May God preserve Your Excellency many years.

CANALEJAS Y MÉNDEZ.

MADRID, *March 16, 1889.*
(*Gaceta* of March 17.)

Royal order of March 19, 1889, on the filling of vacancies of the judicial and the public prosecution services in the first series of succession.

YOUR EXCELLENCY: The first series, which for filling vacancies has been reserved by the additional law to the organic law on judicial power for officers holding the first place in the graded lists, has been granted, up to the present time, indiscriminately and without subjection to rules among those occupying this coveted place in the judicial or the public prosecution services, it having been frequently the case that by virtue of this privilege promotion has been awarded to officers with a time of service shorter than that of other officers of the same category and with the same number, although of a different graded list.

In order to procure hereafter in these cases an interpretation of the law that would be more in conformity with the intention of the legislator, and to compensate for unjustifiable postponements in promotions,

Her Majesty (whom God preserve) the Queen, Regent of the Realm, in the name of her august son, Don Alfonso XIII, has decreed the following:

1. That all the vacancies which hereafter correspond to the first series of succession referred to in articles 42, 43, 44, and 45 of the additional law to the organic law on judicial power, shall be filled with officers of the category immediately inferior, who, not having previously renounced in writing their right to promotion, occupy the first place in the graded lists of the judicial or the public prosecution services, and have to their credit the greatest period of time passed in the category or in the service in question, when several officers are equal in all other respects.

2. From the preceding rule are excepted the vacancies which are filled by the Government in conformity with the power granted the same in the third paragraphs of the said articles 44 and 45.

Your Excellency will please make your recommendations for the series of succession by seniority in conformity with these provisions, which I communicate to your excellency by royal order.

May God preserve Your Excellency many years.

CANALEJAS Y MÉNDEZ.

To the Assistant Secretary of this Department.

MADRID, *March 19, 1889.*
(*Gaceta* of March 20.)

———

Royal order of March 23, 1889, on promotions in the judicial and the public prosecution services.

YOUR EXCELLENCY: The most superficial examination of the graded lists shows how easily some officers succeed in reaching the highest grades of promotions, and how, on the other hand, other judges and associate justices of irreproachable service are being retired while holding modest positions, without regard to lengthy services. The column of the graded list destined to show the seniority in the service presents differences of 15 and even 20 years of service between officers in the same category. Such facts tend to discourage the personnel, to dissuade brilliant youths from taking part in competitive examination for entrance in the service, and render favoritism more numerous than is desirable in seeking benefits and prerogatives that should be granted only for acknowledged and absolute merit.

It is true that an inflexible standard of absolute seniority is impracticable in so numerous a personnel coming from such various sources. But if the latitude allowed by the organic law proves to be beneficial in admitting to the highest grades persons of a genuine and acknowledged juridical ability, it does not by any means authorize neglecting under the press of harmful political influences officers of older standing, who, judging from the fact that they are kept in the service, must be considered worthy of their office, or else they should be discharged from the duties for which they are considered incapable.

The royal decree of April 3, 1884, established wise limitations of the discretionary judgment of secretaries (*arbitrio ministerial*), whose maximum limits have been fixed by the organic law and by the additional law, in order that appointments should be exercised within said limits according to the criterion with which the circumstances or personal convictions influence the secretaries in promotions authorized by their signatures.

Granting full appreciation and respect to the high motives which guided the illustrious secretaries to whom the introduction of extensive reforms suggested and on whom perhaps it imposed an ample exercise of the power of appointment, it is high time, until the Cortes of the Kingdom in their high wisdom establish a system of promotions absolutely exempt from favoritism, to restrict recommendations for promotions to narrower limits, even if these empirical changes, though inspired by proper motives, are not ideal and can not be considered a model of perfection.

In making use for filling vacancies in the fourth series of succession of the provisions of the organic law and the additional law to the same, with the wise limitations established by the royal decree of April 3, 1884, there remains sufficient room for the discretionary judgment of the secretaries in order to recognize and recompense exceptional merits with such an excessive advancement that in some graded list preference is apparently given over 100, 180, and even over 224 officers of greater seniority.

In what refers to the second series of vacancies it is beyond doubt that by limiting the recommendations for promotion to the first third of the graded list an adequate opportunity will be left to reward genuine merit, and by combining this privilege of seniority in the category with the privilege inferred from the inscription in the first half of the graded list of absolute seniority in the service the desire to recompense a special merit may be made to harmonize with the rule that by paying a legitimate attention to officers entering modest categories those should not be systematically overlooked who, in conformity with the legal provisions, entered the service through higher categories.

The rules contained in the royal orders of the 12th, 16th, and 19th of March of this year, and in the present royal order, fix the maximum limits to which the secretary authorizing them shall restrict appointments and promotions which he submits to His Majesty in virtue of the recommendations submitted by your excellency, paying more attention to the personal records than to constant recommendations, born of the harmful prevalence of the desire to give favorable statements, even if they are not justified by facts. The first series of vacancies shall be, as the law commands, reserved strictly to the officers occupying the first places in the graded lists of their categories; the third series of vacancies shall be awarded for seniority in the service, thus compensating for long delays of promotion, and the second series of vacancies shall be filled with officers occupying the first third of the graded list of their category and the first half of their order of succession, in conformity with the graded list of absolute seniority, ordered drafted by the royal order of the 16th of the current March.

In virtue of the considerations stated above, Her Majesty (whom God preserve), Queen Regent of the Realm, in the name of her august son, the King, Don Alfonso XIII, has decreed that the second series of vacancies included in articles 41, 42, 43, 44, and 45 of the additional law occurring hereafter shall be filled with officers of the immediately inferior category who possess all the other qualifications required by the provisions in force and occupy places included in the first third of the graded list of their category and in the first half of the register of absolute seniority in the service, drawn for said category by the royal order of the 16th of March of the current year.

I communicate this to Your Excellency by royal order for your observance in making the proper recommendations.

May God preserve Your Excellency many years.

OANALEJAS Y MÉNDEZ.

To the Assistant Secretary of this Department.
MADRID, *March 23, 1889.*

(*Gaceta*, March 24.)

———

Royal order of August 24, 1889, on the reinstatement of suspended officers in the judicial and the public prosecution services.

In the proceedings instituted for determining the form in which suspended officers may reenter active service in the judicial and the public prosecution services, Her Majesty the Queen (whom God preserve), Regent of the Realm, in the name of her august son, the King, Don Alfonso XIII, in conformity with the report of the section of state, grace, and justice of the council of state, has deemed proper to order that suspended officers desiring to reenter the service shall solicit their reinstatement witin the period of one month, which can not be extended, counting from the date. When said period has elapsed, the respective proceedings shall be transmitted to the board created by the royal decree of February 6, 1888, and if the qualifications of the petitioners for reinstatement in the active service has been declared, they shall be included in the proper place of their graded list.

I communicate the above by royal order to Your Excellency for your information and consequent effect.

May God preserve Your Excellency many years.

OANALEJAS Y MÉNDEZ.

To the Assistant Secretary of this Department.
MADRID, *August 24, 1889.*

(*Gaceta*, August 25.)

———

Royal decree of September 24, 1889, establishing certain guaranties of judicial irremovability and rules for promotions and transfers.

STATEMENT.

MADAM: The guaranties of irremovability established by the organic law on judicial power protect only at the present time the officers entering the service by means of a competitive examination, so that more than four-fifths of our judges and associate justices may be discharged, suspended, and transferred without even a statement of reasons. If to this evil we add the fact that promotions in the second, third, and fourth series permit, without requiring public account nor previous investigation, to dispose of the future of officers by granting a rapid advancement or by constantly delaying it, we find the cause for so many complaints made incessantly in the Parliament and in the press. It is therefore not to be wondered at that the secretary of grace and justice scarcely has time to serve the nation in affairs of a higher importance, as he is daily a victim of hundreds of recommendations forcing him to misuse his discretionary judgment in favor of the persons recommending, and is impeded from exercising them to the benefit of the public service.

The undersigned secretary does not defend the principle of absolute seniority, especially when so heterogeneous a personnel of widely varying origin is in question; he is aware of the fact that an absolute irremovability may sometimes sanction the basest of tyrannies, lowering at the same time all judicial discipline; he does not intend to infringe by departmental measures the resolution of the Cortes of the Kingdom of such important problems; he does not procure a tardy remedy for these evils, as from the beginning of the performance of his duties in this respect he has restricted the appointments of the second, third, and fourth series of succession by the most extreme rules. Other secretaries are at liberty to modify the criterion and standard of conduct, and to request of Your Majesty a repeal of the project of a decree attached thereto, if, according to their principles of government, they deem such action necessary.

The undersigned secretary believes that the most correct interpretation of the law attributes to the exercise of the discretion of the secretary in promotions its natural limits in the interest of the administration of justice and in the recompense of acknowledged and exceptional merits of an officer promoted. It is probable that in exercising these powers of the secretary, action has almost always resulted without taking into account other less acceptable reasons. Among the mistakes never intentionally committed, those committed by the undersigned secretary are perhaps most numerous. But without looking backward, and turning our eyes to the improvement in the future, it is impossible for us not to acknowledge that publication of appointments and information referring to officers is a due tribute to the principle of publicity of departmental acts, characteristic of our system of government, whose natural complement is based on exposing to public opinion the grounds for preference which otherwise, if founded on reasons carefully reserved by the secretary, may serve as a pretext for murmurs of discontent which it is important to prevent in all services, including the judiciary, and, what is more important, for the loss of that inward satisfaction which is an impulse of such noble actions and heroic sacrifices.

Without acknowledged merits, appraised by independent standards, and without an irreproachable record of service, every preference savors of injustice, and the seniority comes forward claiming its sway; only in the highest category a legal tradition supported by valid reasons and deep-rooted practices justifies more amplitude in appointing, even if the undersigned secretary is disposed and considers himself obliged not to go beyond the first third of the inferior graded list.

The confidence which the Government of Your Majesty places in the superior courts, against whose reports no transfers or promotion shall be decreed, and the irremovability of all judges and associate justices until a new law shall make a final decision concerning officers entering the service without a competitive examination, would prove dangerous expansions of a past romanticism, with the result that the judicial organism would lack the necessary energies checking the injustice from above and the iniquity from below.

After having their authority increased, after having their disciplinary self-government initiated under the supreme inspection of the Government, the chambers of administration would disappoint the expectations of the undersigned secretary, showing him ingratitude if they do not help him in expelling the vicious elements in rewarding the other officers, who are the honor and glory of our judiciary. All social organisms reach the grade of development and independence which they conquer; if judicial officers believe that they only fulfill their duties conscientiously, without paying attention to the damage which may be caused to the prestige of the corps by their colleagues whose faults may become public and are not tried and punished in due legal proceedings; if reports on the personnel are subject to partiality for sentimental reasons; if the chambers of administration do not punish with a strong hand the abuse of so many petitions for transfers requested for reasons of convenience often based on feigned sickness; if irremovability is employed as a means of oppression, taken avail of by judges interested in local strifes in favor of their patrons, it shall be necessary to subject the discipline and management of promotions to the discretionary judgment of the secretary.

The undersigned secretary does not expect such alternative, and if he were afraid of it, he would not seek at the price of so painful disappointments a popularity for the Government of which he forms part. Intrusting to the courts themselves the discipline of the employees, conferring upon them the high mission of securing the irremovability of judges without causing damage to justice, seeking in the decisions a certain criterion for promotions in series of appointments, submitting voluntary transfers and changes to the report of hierarchical superiors, the undersigned secretary does not think that want of authority and independence in superior courts can be alleged, and he is confident that under such conditions said courts must answer to the expectations of the Government. whose sole aim is to raise the solemnity of justice and to invigorate the independence and liability of those upon whom society has conferred this pure treasure of social wealth for administration.

In virtue of these considerations, with the approval of the council of secretaries, the undersigned secretary has the honor to submit for the approval of Your Majesty the accompanying project of a decree.

At the royal feet of Your Majesty.

JOSÉ CANALEJAS Y MÉNDEZ.

SAN SEBASTIÁN, *September 23, 1889.*

ROYAL DECREE.

In view of the reasons assigned by the secretary of grace and justice, with the approval of my council of secretaries, in the name of my august son, the King, Don Alfonso XIII, and as Queen Regent of the realm, I decree the following:

ART. 1. Until a new law establishes definitely the guarantees of judicial irremovability and determines the conditions with which judicial officers entering the service otherwise than by means of a competitive examination must comply, in order to enjoy the privilege, no judge or associate justice can be declared suspended or discharged except for cause and with the requisites established in the organic law on judicial power of September 15, 1870, now in force.

ART. 2. The judicial officers who have not entered the service by competitive examination may be transferred only subject to the following rules:

First. By virtue of administrative proceedings in view of the exigencies of the service, and in conformity with the report made in each case by the chamber of administration of the respective territorial audiencias, in cases relating to judges of examination and of first instance, and associate justices of criminal and territorial audiencias, or of the chamber of administration of the supreme court, in the cases relating to presiding judges of chambers of territorial audiencias.

Second. Upon the request of the officers concerned, provided the report referred to in the preceding rule is favorable.

Third. Through exchange, the advisability of which shall be reported on by the chambers of administration of territorial audiencias, or by the supreme court, respectively.

ART. 3. The transfers and exchanges referred to in the rules of the preceding article shall, in addition, be subject to the incompatibilities established by the legislation in force, and no transfer or changes solicited can be allowed until one year has elapsed from the date of the last appointment or transfer.

ART. 4. In the cases of exchanges or transfers granted upon the petition of the officer concerned, the period allowed for taking possession of the office can be extended. In transfers granted in virtue of the administrative proceedings treated of in rule 1 of article 2, the extension granted shall not exceed thirty days. In either case, it shall be construed that the officer resigns the office for which he has been appointed if he fails to take possession of it within the respective periods allowed for taking possession, and does not give justifiable reasons for his inability to do so, in conformity with the provisions of article 187 of the organic law on judicial power.

ART. 5. The vacancies in the judicial and the public prosecution services, corresponding to the first series of succession established by articles 41, 42, 43, 44, and 45 of the additional law to the organic law on judicial power, shall be filled with officers of the category immediately inferior who have not previously filed a written renunciation of their right to promotion, and who occupy the first place in the respective graded lists, and are credited with the greatest length of service in their category. Other conditions being equal, the preference shall be granted to the officer of the greatest seniority in the service. There shall be excepted from this provision the vacancies which are filled by the Government by virtue of the powers that are granted to it by the third paragraphs of articles 44 and 45 of the said law.

ART. 6. In filling vacancies of the second series of succession established by the law, up to the category of associate justices of territorial audiencias, inclusive, preference shall be given to officers who have to their credit the merits mentioned in article 170 of the organic law on judicial power. To carry this provision into effect the persons concerned shall apply to the department of grace and justice in the manner and with the documents specified in article 169 of the said law. The department shall forward the proceedings to the qualification board (*junta calificadora*) of the judicial power, in order that the latter, in view thereof and the judgment of the officer, decides whether he can concur or not in the declaration of merits. After the former have been returned, if the resolution of the board is favorable, and in no other case, they shall be transmitted for report to the corporation or superior court designated by the Government in cases 1, 2, and 3 of the said article 170, and to the council of state in the case referred to in No. 4 of the same article. The bureau of the personnel of the said department shall open and keep a register, in which a memorandum shall be duly made of the officers receiving favorable qualifications. The Government shall appoint freely from among said officers, provided that in each case the appointee possesses the other legal qualifications required for promotion.

ART. 7. If there are no officers who have duly qualified merit for promotion in the second series of succession as described in the preceding article, promotion shall be granted to those who are recommended officially by chambers of boards of administration of audiencias in the reports which are for this purpose demanded of them by the department of grace and justice, or in the recommendations duly accounted for, which may be submitted by said chambers or boards, whenever an officer of their territory in their opinion deserves promotion. In the promotions granted in virtue of the provisions of this and the preceding article special mention shall be made of the merits on which the appointment is based, and the decision shall be published in full, or, if the text is very long, in a summarized form, in order that it may afford a legitimate satisfaction to the officer promoted and a noble stimulus to his colleagues.

ART. 8. In order to fill the vacancies, the provision of which should be effected by the third series of succession, in the categories referred to in articles 41 and 45, inclusive, of the additional law to the organic law, appointments shall be given to officers of the class immediately below who possess the qualifications for promotion required by the legislation in force and who, in addition, have to their credit the greatest number of years in the service and have no unfavorable memorandum in their personal record.

ART. 9. The vacancies corresponding to the fourth series of succession shall be filled in the manner prescribed in article 6 of the present decree for the second series of succession, but this action shall be taken only in the case when the Government does not make use of the power given it by the additional law for granting appointments to the persons designated by the same and without prejudice to the legal provisions in force concerning the suspended officers of the judiciary and the department of public prosecution and the officers serving in the same branches in the colonies.

ART. 10. The provisions on the irremovability of officers of the judicial service contained in the preceding articles shall be enforced from the publication of this decree without prejudice to the resolutions offered by the report of the qualification board of the judicial power, which shall continue as speedily as possible the examination of the personal records referred to in rule 3, article 1, of the royal decree of February 6, 1888.

ART. 11. All the former provisions which conflict with the present decree are hereby repealed.

Given at San Sebastián on September 24, 1889.

MARÍA CRISTINA.

JOSÉ CANALEJAS Y MENDEZ,
Secretary of Grace and Justice.

(*Gaceta* of September 30.)

Royal order of December 16, 1889, on the filling of vacancies in the judicial and the public prosecution services.

As it is frequently the case in filling vacancies in the judicial and the public-prosecution services that there are no officers possessing the legal qualifications for promotion, and in order to establish a general standard to be observed in the future, the King (whom God preserve), and in his name the Queen Regent of the Realm, has decreed the reestablishment in full force of article 11 of the royal order of May 29, 1885, which provides that if in one or more series of succession no officers are found possessing the required qualifications for the office to be filled, said series of succession shall be passed over, and a memorandum to this effect entered in the proper book, while the vacancy shall be filled from the series of succession next in order.

I communicate the above to you by royal order for your information and other effects.

May God preserve you many years.

BECERRA.

MADRID, *December 16, 1889.*

To the Governors-General of Cuba, Puerto Rico, and the Philippines, and to the Director-General of Grace and Justice of this Department.

Royal decree of March 28, 1890, reorganizing the secretary's office of the codification commission of the colonial provinces.

Upon the recommendation of the secretary of the colonies, in the name of my august son, the King, Don Alfonso XIII, and as Queen Regent of the Realm, I decree the following:

ART. 1. The duties of secretary of the codification commission for the colonial provinces shall be performed by the chief of the bureau of civil matters and legislative reforms of the general direction of grace and justice of the colonial department and by the personnel detailed to that bureau.

ART. 2. The provisions of the royal decree of February 25, 1887, reorganizing the said commission, shall remain in force in all matters which do not conflict with the provisions of this decree.

Given at the palace on March 28, 1890.

MARÍA CRISTINA.

MANUEL BECERRA,
Secretary of the Colonies.

Royal decree of October 13, 1890, reestablishing the assimilation of the employees of the general direction of grace and justice and other officers of the department, to whom such assimilation is due, with the officers of the judicial service.

By virtue of the reasons stated to me by the secretary of the colonies I decree the following:

ART. 1. The positions of the personnel of the colonial department belonging to the general direction of said department, up to the third class of officers of administration, auxiliary officers of the secretary's office of the fifth class, inclusive, shall be considered as of officers of the judiciary, serving in commission, with all the privileges that may in this respect be accorded them. Consequently the persons discharging said offices shall have the respective category and grades, shall be granted the same rights of seniority, and shall obtain the same credit for their services which would be granted them if their services were actually rendered in inferior and superior courts of the colonies.

ART. 2. For the assimilation of administrative and judicial categories, in consequence of the provisions of the preceding article, the following equivalents are established:

Chiefs of administration of the first class, officials of the senior secretary's office, shall have the same rank as the associate justices of the audiencia of Habana.

Chiefs of administration of the second and third class, officials of the secretary's office of the first and second class, as the associate judges of territoral audiencias outside of Habana.

Chiefs of administration of the fourth class and chiefs of bureaus of the first class, officials of the secretary's office of the third class, and auxiliaries of senior secretaries' offices, respectively, as associate justices of criminal audiencias.

Chiefs of bureaus of the second class, auxiliaries of the first grade, as judges of the final category.

Chiefs of bureaus of the third class and first-grade officials of administration, auxiliaries of the second and third classes, as judges of the promotion category.

Second and third grade officials of administration, auxiliaries of the secretaries' offices of the fourth and fifth grades, as judges of the entrance category.

The categories above enumerated shall be understood as acquired by analogy in their equivalents of the department of public prosecution.

ART. 3. An officer of the direction, who shall be transferred with or without a promotion to the judicial and the public-prosecution services in the colonial provinces can not return to the direction without having held his office in the inferior or superior courts of those provinces for an uninterrupted period of two years.

ART. 4. A change for executive offices of those in the judicial and public-prosecution services in the colonies can be decreed only in making use of the fourth series established by the royal decree issued by the department of this branch on the 26th of October, 1888.

ART. 5. The officers attached to the general direction of grace and justice of the colonial department up to the category of official of administration of the third class, inclusive, shall enjoy the benefits granted by this decree, and the following rules shall be applied for carrying out the provisions of article 2.

First. Those who have acquired a judicial category higher than that of the office they fill shall preserve said category with all the rights granted therewith in the order conferring the office.

Second. Those having a category inferior to that of the office which they fill shall obtain the category belonging to that office, acquiring it for all legal effects, after having served two years in the inferior category.

Third. For the personnel to which a judicial category has not been granted, and which served in the general direction of grace and justice at the date of the promulgation of the budget law now in force, issued for the island of Cuba and for the personnel of the aforesaid general direction before the publication of this decree, the assimilation to the judicial service of the colonies is hereby reestablished and carried into effect at once under the conditions and in the form established by the decree of May 2, 1869, and by the royal decree of April 12, 1875.

ART. 6. The assimilation reestablished by the third rule of the preceding article does not grant the right to enter into the judicial or the public-prosecution services of the peninsula, nor to appear in a certain category in the united graded lists for the branches of the service in the peninsula and the colonies, until the persons obtaining assimilation comply with the requirements fixed in article 7 of this decree.

ART. 7. The officers who at the time this decree is published are attached to the general direction of grace and justice may acquire the judicial category corresponding to the office which they fill when they possess or comply with the following requisites:

First. Of having reached the age of 25 years and being a lawyer.

Second. Of having served the number of years which the additional law on judicial power, promulgated for the Peninsula, requires of lawyers for obtaining by the fourth series of succession an equal position in superior or inferior courts. The time spent in law practice shall be taken into account.

Third. Of having to their credit among these services at least four years of service in the direction of grace and justice of the colonial department.

ART. 8. In conceding assimilation of rank that may belong to officers who may in the future be attached to the direction of grace and justice of the colonial department, proceedings shall be instituted in each case, in which said requirements and the qualifications of aptitude of the officer seeking the assimilation shall be duly demonstrated.

ART. 9. Officials of administration of the fourth and fifth classes, and auxiliaries of the sixth and the seventh classes serving in the general direction of grace and justice, shall in no case be considered as assimilated to the judicial service.

ART. 10. For the purposes of assimilation the personnel of the general direction of grace and justice of the colonial department shall include the categories, classes, and number of officers established, as follows:

One chief of administration of the first class.
One chief of administration of the second class.
One chief of administration of the third class.
Two chiefs of administration of the fourth class.
Two chiefs of bureaus of the first class.
Three chiefs of bureaus of the second class.
Three chiefs of bureaus of the third class.
Three first grade officials of administration.
Eight second grade officials of administration.
Two third grade officials of administration.

And the number of officials of the fourth and fifth grades and of candidates that are considered necessary for the efficacy of the service.

Given at San Sebastián on October 13, 1890.

MARÍA CRISTINA.

ANTONIO MARIA FABIÉ,
 Secretary of the Colonies.

Decree-law of October 13, 1890, on entrance, transfers, and promotion of officers of the general administration of the State in the colonial possessions.

In view of the reasons stated to me by the secretary of the colonies, I decree the following:

CHAPTER I.

EMPLOYEES.

ART. 1. In the provisions of this decree-law shall be considered included the officers of the general administration of state in the colonial department and its peninsular dependencies, and those of the provinces subject to the rule and government of said department, whose services are not regulated by special provisions.

ART. 2. The employees to whom the preceding article refers may aspire, according to their respective abilities, to the administrative categories and classes, recognized by the provisions in force in the Peninsula, and to the salaries fixed by the general budget laws for the colonies, and the extra pay fixed by the same laws for offices in the colonial provinces.

ART. 3. The colonial department shall draft two general graded lists, one including all the employees of royal appointment in the actual service of the general administration of state, either in the department and its peninsular dependencies, or in the colonial possessions; and another, including the discharged officers who served in the administration of State above referred to.

The office of the assistant secretary of this department shall also draft two other graded lists which shall contain the subordinate personnel, active as well as passive, of the said branch of service and its peninsular dependencies.

The same shall be done by the governors-general of the colonial provinces with regard to the subordinate personnel depending on said governors and the other authorities of the state in the territory intrusted to them, and shall forward to the department copies of both graded lists.

ART. 4. Employees belonging to services or bodies organized by special provisions or laws shall continue to be governed thereby in so far as they are not modified by the present decree law or other special provisions.

The provisions included in this decree law shall have a supplementary character in all the cases not provided for in the exceptional provisions governing said employees.

Should any of said services or bodies be abolished or dissolved the employees of the same shall be included in the general graded list of discharged officers of the general administration of state of the colonies, and their category and class shall be computed on the basis of the amount of personal salary which they received.

ART. 5. The employees of special bodies or branches of service who obtain an employment included in the graded lists of active officers of the general administration of state in the department and its dependencies, in the Peninsula and in the colonies, shall be kept on the graded list of their respective branches of service or bodies, and may return to the employment in the same in the cases and under the conditions authorized by the provisions governing said employment.

ART. 6. In the future no special branch of service shall be organized except by a bill of law voted upon in the Cortes.

ART. 7. The appointments of officers belonging to the category of a superior chief of administration, or of chief of administration, shall be made by means of a royal decree; those of chiefs of bureaus and of officers of administration by a royal order; appointments of subordinate officers by the assistant secretary's office of the department and by the superior colonial authorities within the limit of the powers granted to each of them.

ART. 8. In each appointment a statement shall be made of the category and class of the office and of the legal qualifications of the appointee and the series of succession to which the appointment corresponds.

ART. 9. The superior chiefs of administration and the civil governors of the colonial provinces, who from other considerations have no right to be included in the graded lists with the categories and classes of said officers, shall not enter said categories or classes until they have been filling the same for two years, deducting the time of leave, office or offices corresponding to the respective category and class.

Should the time of service in a higher category or class be insufficient to include the officer in question in the same on the graded list, that time shall be added to the period of service in inferior categories or classes, as the time spent in actual service in the latter categories or classes, and shall give to said officers the privilege of occupying a higher place among the employees of the same class.

CHAPTER II.

ENTRANCE.

ART. 10. Entrance and promotion into the service of the general administration of State in the department and its Peninsular dependencies and in the colonial provinces shall be adjusted to the following rules, however without prejudice to the other provisions established by the present decree law:

1. Suspended officers may return to active service in an employment of the same category and class as that which they filled previously.

2. No office can be entered except through the fifth class of officers of administration. Persons holding academic or professional degrees or having pursued higher studies may enter the service as officers of administration of the second class.

3. For promotion from one class to another two years of service in the class immediately inferior are required, besides a proportionate number of years spent in the service of the State according to the following scale:

For promotion to chief of administration, ten years; for promotion to chief of bureau, eight; for officers of administration of the first class, five; for officers of administration of the second class, four; for officers of administration of the third class, three; and for officers of administration of the fourth class, two.

The officers of the civil and economic administration of state holding academic degrees of higher studies or professions may be promoted to officers of administration of the first class after completing two years of service as officers of the second class, and to chiefs of bureaus of the third class after completing two years of service as officers of the first class.

ART. 11. To obtain the office of a superior chief of administration the candidate is required to be or to have been a senator or deputy to the

Cortes during the period of two general elections; to have to his credit ten years of service in the civil administration, or to have drawn a salary equal to or higher than that of 8,750 pesetas.

ART. 12. To be appointed governor of a province in the island of Cuba or in the Philippine archipelago, when military authority over the territory is not vested in said office, the following qualifications are required:

1. To have filled for any time offices with the category of chief of administration of the first class, or to have filled for more than one year offices with the category of chiefs of administration of the second class, or for more than two years similar offices of the third or of the fourth class.

2. To be credited with more than fifteen years of administrative service in the State or in the province, provided that the last office has been of a category higher than that of a chief of bureau of the third class.

3. To have been a deputy to the Cortes or to have been an elected senator during one full term of the legislature.

4. To have been elected a provincial deputy at least twice, and to have taken possession and filled said office without leaving it by resignation.

5. To have been an associate justice of any audiencia or *teniente fiscal* for a period of more than two years, or to have filled an office in the judicial service higher than the two above mentioned.

6. To have filled the office of alcalde in the regular manner for more than two years in capitals of provinces of the first or second class, or to have been a member of a provincial commission for the same length of time.

7. To have been secretary of administration for more than two years in first-class provinces.

8. To be or to have been a secretary appointed through a competitive examination in a provincial deputation of first-class provinces for the period of four years.

Appointments to be governors of provinces may also be given to soldiers who have spent twenty-five years in the military service, ten of which in the actual service as commanders; and in the Philippine Islands persons who are or have been political military governors in said territory for two years with the minimum rank of major of the army or its equivalent in the naval service, and to those who for an equal period of time have served until the publication of the Royal decree of March 5, 1886, in the capacity of mayors (*alcalde mayor*) with the category of judge of first instance of the promotion or of the final category.

If the Government learns that any of the colonial provinces is subject to circumstances requiring special precautions for the sake of national unity, or in such an abnormal condition that special qualifications are necessary to satisfy the exigencies of its government, and when it is thought that there are no persons among the officers referred to in this article possessing the necessary ability for the case, the office of the governor of said province may be conferred upon a person of acknowledged fitness and patriotism after the approval of the council of secretaries, which shall decide upon the advisability of adopting such measures.

ART. 13. Residents of the islands of Cuba, Puerto Rico, and the Philippines who have been discharging duties as provincial deputy, as alcalde, or as member of the council in the capital of a province, or who have belonged in the capacity of members of administrative councils or of the existing consultive or auxiliary boards of administration of a central character, may be appointed chiefs of administration of any class and in the administrative service of the respective provinces, except in the custom-house service. For the offices of chiefs of bureaus of the said territories in similar circumstances the appointment may be given to persons who have belonged to the provincial and local boards of that same class, or who have been *alcaldes* or councilmen of a municipality which is not a capital, provided that said persons possess the following qualifications:

Of having resided in the territory in question for eight years previous to appointment.

Of having discharged for the period of four years any of the offices enumerated in this article without having resigned from the same.

Of having discharged in a proper case the duties of a provincial deputy, alcalde, or councilman, by virtue of a popular election.

ART. 14. The legal qualifications stated in the preceding article for offices of chiefs of administration, or chiefs of bureaus, does not grant under any circumstances the privilege of seeking employment of a higher or inferior category.

The time spent in service in the capacity of a provincial deputy, member of a provincial commission, alcalde, or councilman, by virtue of a Government appointment, shall not be taken into account for the acknowledgment of said legal qualifications.

Said legal qualifications shall be shown by documents in proceedings before the appointments are made.

The appointees shall not be entered in the general graded lists until after they have served in the offices conferred on them for two years, deducting the time taken for leave, except when they have a right to be included in the graded list for other causes.

ART. 15. The admission to the service of the general administration of state in the colonial provinces, with the category of officer of administration of the third or fourth classes, may be granted to the persons possessing all of the qualifications mentioned below:

To be at least 21 years of age.

To have a degree of bachelor of arts.

To have studied and have been certified in having successfully passed in official universities the courses of political law, administrative law, political economy, public treasury, and obtained in said courses a standing of a grade higher than the grade "Passed."

To have studied and have been certified in having successfully passed at the Central University a course on colonization endowed by the colonial department, and obtained in said course a standing of a grade higher than the grade "Passed."

Appointment shall not be granted until due certification is made with proper documents proving the above qualifications.

ART. 16. The appointment of officers of the fifth class of the department and its peninsular dependencies shall be granted to persons who, besides being at least 20 years of age, possess the following qualifications:

Of having discharged creditably a similar office in the public administration, or having filled for two years the office of a candidate in the same manner, or holding the degree of bachelor of arts, or a professional degree of any other kind.

ART. 17. Appointment of officers of the fifth class in the colonial provinces shall be made by the respective governors-general, who shall immediately report on the matter to the department, in order that said appointments may be confirmed by a Royal order.

The appointment shall be made with a statement of qualifications of the appointee, said qualifications being duly proven to the department by the proper documents.

The following shall be the qualifications:

1. Residence in the territory in question for two years prior to the date of appointment.

2. To be at least 18 years of age.

3. To have creditably discharged a similar office in any dependency of the central or provincial administration, or to have filled creditably subordinate offices as a candidate or clerk with similar good conduct, with a minimum annual salary during four years, amounting to 300 pesos in Puerto Rico and the Philippines, and 600 pesos in Cuba, or holding a degree of bachelor of arts, or a professional degree of any kind.

ART. 18. The secretary of the colonies need not approve an appointment if there are grounds for such action, but the appointee shall draw the salary for the time during which he has filled his office.

The denial of approval shall duly give the reasons therefor, and shall be binding, relative to drawing salary, eight days after the corresponding order has been received in the General Government.

In the latter case the appointment of a governor-general shall be without legal effect for the computation of the length of service or for the granting of a category.

ART. 19. Any appointment of an officer of the fifth class made by a governor-general of persons who have not previously shown the qualifications required by article 17, shall be considered null, and any salary that has been paid to such appointees before they have proven their qualifications, shall be charged to the disbursing officers.

ART. 20. The royal order confirming the appointment of an officer of the fifth class shall have a retroactive legal effect to the date on which the appointment was made by the governor-general.

ART. 21. The appointments to the positions of treasurers-general of the treasury, provincial treasurers, depositaries and collectors of the treasury branch of service, of any class and category, shall be made by the colonial secretary at the suggestion of the respective governors-general with the approval of the *intendentes*.

The persons who possess the qualifications specified in article 10 of this decree, and who, besides, offer and execute the bond required for the office, shall be recommended for appointment.

Recommendations for appointment shall be accompanied by documents certifying that the above requirements have been complied with.

Said appointments shall not be included within the order of the series of succession established by article 25.

ART. 22. In order to properly fill the offices of candidates, clerks, and other subordinate employees of administrative offices, the respective governors-general shall draft and recommend to the colonial department the proper regulations, designating the offices to be filled by each authority in the territory subject to their jurisdiction, and providing that one-third of said offices be given to the persons who have been discharged from the army or the navy with a good record of military service and who have settled in the country.

ART. 23. The employees and subordinate officers of the public order or of the police shall be appointed without restriction by the governors-general, but shall not enjoy the benefits conferred by this decree-law.

The same rule shall be applied to employees of the garrison, with the exception of chiefs of garrison establishments, who shall be appointed by the secretary of the colonies, outside of the series of succession, but subject to the requirements necessary to solicit employment of the same category and class as that granted to the commanding chiefs of colonial garrisons.

ART. 24. Until otherwise decreed, entrance and promotions of civil officers serving in the Spanish possession of the Gulf of Guinea shall be by means of an unrestricted selection. In order to be included in the general graded list and to enjoy the privilege conferred by this decree-law, two years of actual service with permanent residence in the colony shall be required of officers of administration in the last category, and four years of chiefs of bureaus, or in all, six years of actual service with a permanent residence in the colonies, the time of leaves of absence being deducted.

Officers of any class or category who are accompanied in these colonies by their wives or children shall enjoy during their residence in the colonies an increase of 10 per cent of their total salary.

CHAPTER III.

PROMOTIONS AND VACANCIES.

ART. 25. Entrance as well as promotions in the service of the general administration of state in the colonial department and its peninsula and colonial dependencies shall be adjusted, besides the provisions contained in the preceding chapter, to the following series of succession:

1. Of seniority among active employees.
2. Of seniority among suspended officers.
3. Of selection among active employees.
4. Of selection among suspended officers.
5. Of unrestricted appointment with the conditions fixed for entrance in the preceding chapter and in article 10 of this decree-law.

ART. 26. In the first series of succession promotions shall be given to the active employees occupying the first places in the classes immediately inferior to that in which the vacancy occurs, up to officers of the fifth class, inclusive.

ART. 27. In the second series of succession, appointments shall be given to the suspended officers who hold the category and class equal to that of the office to be filled and occupy the first place in the respective graded list.

Should there be no candidates holding the category and class of the vacancy, the appointment shall be bestowed on the persons of the category and class immediately below, who occupy the first place and have to their credit two years of actual service in the same.

Should there also be no such candidates, the series of succession shall be declared to be passed over and the vacancy shall be filled by the third series.

ART. 28. In the third series the appointment may be granted to an active employee included in the category and class immediately inferior to that of the vacancy, and possessing the following qualifications:

1. Of being included in the first half of the list of officers of his class.
2. Of having to his credit two years of service in his class.
3. Of having to his credit the full number of years that are required by article 10 of this decree-law for the various administrative categories.
4. Of being at the time of appointment in the locality of his office.

Appointments in this series of succession to serve in the colonial provinces and possessions beyond the sea, may also be granted to officers of the civil administration in the peninsula or of the colonial department and its dependencies in Madrid, to whom shall be granted promotion, without regard to the time of service in their category and class, and with two promotions if they lack less than six months of being qualified for promotion in the Peninsula by selection.

ART. 29. In the fourth series of succession appointment may be granted to a suspended officer appearing in the graded list in the category and class equal to those of the vacancy, or else with the ones immediately inferior.

In the latter case the suspended officer must have the following qualifications:

1. He must be included in the first half of the list of officers of his class.

2. He must have to his credit two years of service in his class.

3. He must have to his credit the full number of years which are prescribed by article 10 of this decree law as a qualification for seeking appointment in the various categories.

Preference shall be given to suspended officers possessing the above qualifications to those who have been suspended with pay, and, in their default, to officers suspended on account of abolition of their offices, or on account of reforms.

Appointment in this series of succession for offices in the colonial provinces and possessions may be granted also to suspended officers of the civil administration of the Peninsula, or of the colonial department and its dependencies in Madrid; and a promotion shall be conceded them without regard to the time which they have to their credit in their class and category, and with two promotions if less than six months are lacking for their reinstatement with promotion in the Peninsula.

ART. 30. In the fifth series of promotions vacancies shall be filled in the following manner:

If the vacancy is of a category inferior to that of a superior chief of administration and of a higher category and class than those of an official of administration of the second class, the appointment shall be granted to an active or passive officer of the general administration of state in the Peninsula, or of the colonial department and its dependencies in Madrid, or of special branches of the service or bodies which belong to the class immediately inferior to that of the vacancy or to its equivalent in a special branch of the service or a special body, no regard being paid to the length of time spent by said officer in the class in question. Appointment may also be made of officers of the same branches of the service who have filled an office inferior by two classes or grades, and who have to their credit one year and a half in the service. In either case the full number of years of service shall be required, as prescribed by article 10 of this decree law, for a transfer from one category to another.

If an office of administration of the second, third, or fourth class is vacant, it shall be filled in the manner described in the preceding paragraph, or else the appointment shall be given to persons possessing the qualifications which are required by articles 10 and 15 of this decree law for aspiring to said categories and classes, although the persons in question have either never been employed by the State, or have discharged duties of an inferior class.

The advantages obtained by virtue of what is authorized in this article and in the two articles immediately preceding it shall not be considered as granted with an office, so far as the colonial provinces are concerned, until the office obtained shall have been filled for two years, deduction being made for leaves of absence.

After this condition shall have been complied with by the employee, he may be transferred with the category and class he has acquired to the general administration of state of the Peninsula or to the colonial department or its dependencies in Madrid.

ART. 31. If any member of the council of state, either active or suspended, is appointed without retaining his membership in the council to fill the office of a superior chief of administration in the colonies, he shall draw 3,000 pesetas of salary fixed for the office, which salary shall not be affected by the total amount provided for in the budget.

ART. 32. The personal salary drawn, or the highest salary which has been drawn by an officer from a special branch of the service or body who is about to be appointed to fill an office in the civil administration of the colonies, shall serve as a basis for granting to said officer the category and class belonging to him in accordance with the categories and classes included in the general graded lists of the employees of the general administration of state.

ART. 33. The employees rendering services in the colonial department and its peninsular dependencies may renounce in advance the promotions to offices in the colonies which may belong to them by right of seniority or appointment, said renunciation being made in a request drawn to that effect.

The employees of the Antilles may likewise renounce promotions to offices in the Philippine Islands and *vice versa*.

Should an officer renounce a promotion for any other causes he shall be declared suspended, provided that the office does not require a bond.

ART. 34. Suspended officers who have been given an employment not requiring a bond, or one of a category and class inferior to that of the highest office which they have discharged, and who have renounced or have not taken possession of their office in the time fixed by the regulations, shall appear in their graded list in the last place of their class.

ART. 35. When no candidates are found in the series of succession from which a vacancy should be filled the vacancy shall be filled from the series next in numerical order. When the fifth series of succession is made use of the first series shall be next utilized.

ART. 36. The colonial department may renounce the right to fill vacancies by the fifth series of succession whenever it approves filling said vacancy by the first series.

ART. 37. Claims may be made in administrative litigation by the persons who consider themselves to be wronged by appointments made with modifications of the series established by this decree law, except when such modifications are authorized by the preceding article.

CHAPTER IV.

GRADED LISTS.

ART. 38. In the month of May of the year 1891 the assistant secretary's office of the colonial department shall publish provisionally the two general graded lists referred to in article 3.

Said graded lists shall be binding until the formation of the final ones, to be published on June 30, 1892. The latter shall serve as a basis for the annual ones to be drafted and published thereafter in conformity with article 41.

ART. 39. Employees shall be included in the graded lists within each category and class in strict order of seniority. Public officers in offices inferior to those which they have reached in their careers shall be given the first places in the graded lists of the respective classes in which they appear as in active service. A greater number of years in service, and in cases of equality in this respect, a greater age shall determine the order of preference to be granted to officers of equal seniority.

Graded lists shall not contain lists of employees subject to administrative proceedings or trials before the date of this decree law until said proceedings or trials come to a final decision with a declaration therein authorizing the inclusion of said employees in the graded lists.

ART. 40. After the graded lists are published persons who have a right to be included therein may complain of the place assigned to them in the same, or may request to be included if they have been omitted.

Complaint shall be made within the period of one month by parties residing in the Peninsula, three months by those residing in Cuba and Puerto Rico, and six months by those residing in the Philippines, or in the Spanish possessions in the Gulf of Guinea. After the period assigned for making complaints has elapsed no claim shall be received.

ART. 41. Beginning with the year 1893 annual graded lists shall be published in the month of July of each year, showing the status of the service as it appeared on the 30th of the preceding June.

ART. 42. The colonial department shall issue the necessary regulations in order that the formation of the provisional general graded lists to be published in May, 1891, may be furnished by the higher authorities of the colonial provinces and possessions, and by the active and suspended officers residing in the colonies or in the Peninsula.

CHAPTER V.

SUSPENSIONS.

ART. 43. Suspensions shall be decreed unrestrictedly by the authorities which made the corresponding appointment. The governors-general shall report to the Government on the causes of suspensions decreed by them.

Notwithstanding this provision, the secretary of the colonies may decree the suspension of officers of administration of the fifth class, whose appointment is made by the governors-general, whenever such suspension is demanded by the good of the service of the State.

A suspended officer shall be entered in the proper place in the general graded list of suspended officers.

ART. 44. If a suspension has been caused by serious offenses committed by an employee in the exercise of his duties, he may be reduced in the graded list upon the recommendation of the respective governors-general, after a decision of the jury provided for in article 82, and after the other formalities regulating the procedure of this jury, which are established in articles 82 and 84 of this decree law.

ART. 45. The employees of the public administration who are prosecuted criminally at the instance of some person or otherwise, shall be suspended from their duties from the moment in which said complaint is made. Such officers of the colonial provinces shall have a right to draw only one-fourth of their salary for living expenses, said pay in no case exceeding 1,000 pesos, until a definite decision is rendered.

The pay for living expenses referred to in this article is limited only to the cases where an officer is tried for acts relating to the office which he fills in the territory under the jurisdiction of the colonial courts taking cognizance of the cause, and it shall cease when the officer in question shall have been condemned in any other cause.

ART. 46. After a sentence has been pronounced either condemning or acquitting, or staying proceedings, a decision shall be made in an administrative way after hearing the council of state, upon the standing of the employee, his final reduction or retention in the service, the time of service, and other administrative matters.

CHAPTER VI.

TRANSFERS, EXCHANGES, LEAVES, AND COMMISSIONS OF THE SERVICE.

ART. 47. Every employee of the colonial provinces may be transferred within the islands of Cuba, Puerto Rico, and the Philippines, respectively, to officers of a category and class equal to the category and class of the office which he fills, if the transfer would prove of utility to the service.

Transfers of officers serving in the Antilles to the Philippines and *vice versa* can be made unrestrictedly only for the interest of the service, when the employee to be transferred has completed two years of continuous residence in any of said territories.

ART. 48. Officers are hereby forbidden to discharge duties other than those which properly belong to their regular offices, except in cases of substitution or in case of a greater usefulness to the service. In these cases the governors-general shall recommend the transfer beforehand, which shall in no case be made without the approval of the colonial department; or, if made, the payment of salary which might otherwise be due to the officer transferred, either for his regular or for the incidental duties is prohibited, under the liability of the disbursing officers.

ART. 49. Public officers discharging their duties in the colonial provinces may obtain temporary leaves for Europe, subject to the following rules:

1. It shall be an indispensable condition for requesting leaves to have remained in active service in any of said provinces three consecutive years without interruption.

2. The maximum time of leaves which can not be extended shall be adjusted according to the following scale: In cases of officers who have complied with the condition of the preceding rule, six months for officers of the Philippines and African possessions, or four months for officers of Cuba and Puerto Rico; in cases of officers of the same possessions who have remained in active service as specified in rule 1 for six consecutive years—nine and six months, respectively; in cases of active, uninterrupted service reaching ten consecutive years, twelve months and eight months, respectively, for the former and the latter officers.

3. A leave obtained under any conditions deprives the officer making use of it of the right to request another leave until the conditions specified in rules 1 and 2, as may be the case, have been complied with again.

4. Leaves of absence shall be requested by the parties interested in due form and medium to the secretary of the colonies.

5. Only in cases of serious sickness duly proven, which endangers the life of the employee concerned, can the governors-general advance leaves for Europe for one-half of the time respectively fixed in rule 2, said leaves being granted after due investigation made by the immediate superiors of the employee in question, or, in cases of employees of the treasury. after a recommendation of the *intendente* or director-general of the service.

6. In drafting the papers which show the causes calling for a leave, as well as for the payment of the salary during the time of the leave, according as to whether it has been granted on account of sickness or for personal reasons, the prescriptions of the preceding rule shall be taken into account, and, further, that a leave must invariably be passed upon when the officer requesting it proves his poor health; and that such officer, from the day on which he ceases to perform his duties until the day on which he returns to them, shall draw only the personal salary corresponding to his office.

ART. 50. Leaves for any points in Asia and America that are not included in the colonial provinces shall be granted by the governors-general for a period of forty-five days, with an extension limited to twenty-two days, which may be granted in cases of sickness duly proved; and officers obtaining such leaves shall draw both the pay and the extra pay corresponding to their office.

When leaves of absence are granted for personal reasons, their time shall in no case exceed forty-five days; and an officer making use of such leave shall not draw any salary.

ART. 51. Leaves for points within the same islands in which the colonial officers requesting leaves render their services, shall be granted by the superior authorities concerned, and shall be subject to the following rules:

1. Colonial employees can not absent themselves from the town in which they discharge their special duties without a leave granted them by the competent authorities. An employee absenting himself without leave shall be considered as resigning his office, and shall be declared suspended, without prejudice to the other liabilities that may be incurred.

2. Leaves must be invariably solicited in writing, and through the immediate superior. When solicited on account of sickness a medical certificate must corroborate the statement.

If the proofs presented by an officer in asking for a leave are in the opinion of his immediate superior insufficient, the latter may demand their amplification.

In a petition for a leave the employee soliciting it must mention the leaves which he has enjoyed during the preceding three years.

3. The immediate superior, in passing upon a leave, shall state his opinion on the necessity of the employee to take it, and on the possibility to grant it without prejudice to the service.

4. Leaves on account of sickness shall be granted with full pay for one month only, and with one-half of the pay for fifteen days more. Leaves granted for other reasons shall be without pay.

5. A memorandum shall be made in the record of service and in the personal record of each employee of each leave he takes.

6. An employee obtaining leave every year for three consecutive years, can not obtain another during the next three years.

7. Not more than one-fifth of the personnel of the same office or of the same public service can make use of leaves at the same time.

Chiefs of the dependencies, under their own liability, shall not allow any employee to make use of his leave if the full number of employees allowed are on leave and the employee in question would cause that number to be exceeded.

8. A leave granted to an employee shall be void if said employee is transferred to another office before he makes use of the same, and it shall be necessary to obtain a new order granting a leave to said officer before he can make use of it in his new employment.

ART. 52. Colonial authorities granting leaves to public officers appointed by the department shall make a report to the department on all such leaves, in order that they may be included in the proper personal records.

ART. 53. The period of residence referred to in rules 1 and 2 of article 49 for obtaining leaves shall not be considered as interrupted by the granting of leaves for which said period is fixed, or by a voyage and residence in the Peninsula to which the officers are compelled who, by the decision of the Government, are transferred from the Philippines to Cuba and Puerto Rico, and *vice versa*, or from African possessions to any other colonial provinces.

ART. 54. It is absolutely forbidden to authorize a residence of colonial officers after the period of leave allowed by the regulations has elapsed. The officers transferred from one province to another, according to the statements of the preceding article, may remain in Europe during one month, with a privilege to draw the salary of their new office from the date of their embarkation in the province of their former office, provided they take possession of their new employment.

If this time has elapsed and said officers should not continue their voyage, it shall be construed that they resign their new office, except when they have been authorized by the Government to remain thirty days more on account of sickness, duly proven by proper documents, in which case said officers shall draw their personal salary during the period extended by the authorization.

ART. 55. If officers to whom leaves are granted make a direct voyage to the Peninsula, or any other point of Europe, Asia, or America, the commencement of their leave shall be computed from the day of their landing, which shall be certified to by the captain of the port of landing, or by a Spanish consul, respectively, according as to whether the place of destination is in the Peninsula or outside of it.

If the voyage is not direct, the time of the leave shall be counted from the date of embarkation in the colonial province from which the officer in question has come.

ART. 56. In fulfillment of the obligations which must be complied with by an officer during the time of his leave the following rules shall be observed:

1. Employees making use of leaves must obtain certification of their return embarkation before the expiration of the time allowed in their leaves; this obligation shall be effected by means of a certificate of the captain of the port of embarkation in the Peninsula or by the Spanish consul abroad, from which they begin their voyage.

The date of arrival at the place of their office shall also be certified to by the captain of the port.

Duplicates of both certifications shall be issued, one addressed to the colonial department and the other to the *intendente* or to the director of the treasury of the province in which said officers serve.

2. Any detention or voluntary interruption of the return voyage begun for the purpose of returning to the office, after having enjoyed a leave, shall cause the loss of the employment and of the personal rights acquired.

3. Whenever, at the expiration of the time allowed for leaves, the employees making use of the same have not reembarked for the return voyage to the places of their offices, they shall be declared suspended unless they assign as a cause for such action poor health, duly proved by proper certificates, or any other duly established and legitimate cause, preventing them from returning to the colonial province from which they came.

If any of the two above circumstances is lacking, said officers shall be considered as included in the preceding rule.

In either case said c ?cers shall incur the penalties established in said rule from the date on which the time allowed for the leave has expired.

4. Leaves granted for Europe and between Asia and America shall become void when not made use of within two months after being communicated to the officers concerned. Leaves granted for points within the same island or for neighboring islands, either in the Antilles or in the Philippines, shall become void when not made use of within one month after being communicated to said officers.

Leaves shall likewise become void, without regard to whether the employees to whom they are granted make use of them or not, if said employees obtain new offices.

5. Transportation charges shall in no case be allowed to employees on leaves, without regard to the cause or destination for which said leaves have been granted.

ART. 57. Commissions for the service in the Peninsula shall be conferred only for extraordinary and urgent necessities of the State, accredited by a written communication of the superior colonial authorities if the conferring of the commission comes from said authorities, or in a royal order if it comes from the colonial department.

ART. 58. Said concessions shall be conferred only for an unextendable period of four months, counting from the date of landing at a peninsular port after a direct voyage from the place at which the officer given the commission has been employed, and it may be conferred on *intendentes* or directors of the treasury, directors or subdirectors general of the civil administration, presiding judges of audiencias and *fiscales* of the same, and of local courts of administrative litigation departments, except treasurers and accountants who are intrusted with general services which extend to the whole territory, respectively, of the islands of Cuba, Puerto Rico, and the Philippines, with a right for the entire duration of the commission to the personal salary of the regular office and an extra pay amounting to one-half of that salary, together with traveling expenses both ways, duly proved by the proper vouchers.

ART. 59. Officers coming to the Peninsula from the aforesaid provinces in commission for the service shall, in a note of presentation at the colonial department, certify that they made a direct voyage. If they fail to do so, they shall lose the right to traveling expenses at the expense of the Government and to the salary which is allowed them in the special services in commission, and they incur an obligation to refund to the public treasury the amount advanced to them either for transportation or as salary. In such cases they must make a return voyage to the place of their regular offices within the unextendable period of thirty days, counted from the date of their landing, during which period they shall not draw any salary.

ART. 60. Extraordinary commissions for the service may also in special circumstances be conferred for places within the colonial province in which the employee intrusted with the commission fills an office. If transferred to a place outside of his regular residence, said employee shall have a right to his pay and extra pay and an additional pay amounting to one-half of his total salary for the entire duration of the commission, which shall never exceed three months. He shall also be allowed traveling expenses both ways.

ART. 61. Hereafter no attachment shall be ordered of colonial officers to the colonial department or other peninsular dependency of the administration.

ART. 62. Any officer coming to the Peninsula in violation of the conditions established in this decree, on leave or in commission for the service, even if said leave or commission has been granted through an error or the neglect of his hierarchical superiors, shall be discharged from the service, and the order of the discharge shall have a retroactive effect to the date on which the employee in question ceased to perform the duties of his office.

CHAPTER VII.

TRANSPORTATION AND DATES OF EMBARKATION.

ART. 63. Public officers destined to the colonial provinces, to whatever service they may belong, shall have a right to allowances for transportation both ways for themselves and their families at the expense of the State, in the form and amount fixed by the following articles.

ART. 64. For the purposes of the preceding article those employees are considered as public officers who have been appointed by a royal decree or a royal order, with the exception of officers of administration of the fifth class, and whose salaries are provided for in the general budgets and are paid from the treasuries (*cajas*) of the colonial provinces.

ART. 65. In allowing transportation expenses the following persons shall be considered as constituting the family of an employee: A legitimate wife; legitimate, acknowledged, natural, and adopted children, when not freed from paternal authority; and the widowed mother taken into the house of and maintained by the son.

ART. 66. Transportation charges at the expense of the State for public officers shall be adjusted to the following scale:

In the transportation lines of the Antilles—

1. Full transportation of the first category of the first class for chiefs of administration or their equals in category.

2. Full transportation of the third category of the first class for chiefs of bureaus or their equals.

3. Full transportation of the second category of the first class for officers of administration and their equals.

In the line of the Philippines—

Full transportation of the first class until the chartered company establishes mail steamers in such categories as appear in the rates of the Antilles line.

For Fernando Pö—

Full transportation of the first class in the form actually established.

ART. 67. The superior chiefs of administration and the right reverend archbishops and the very reverend bishops shall be given on board the ships an apartment with three berths besides the one corresponding to the regular passage, it being understood that for the apartment of three berths the chartered company of mail steamers shall be paid one-half of the price fixed in the rates for the public, according to the order of the Regent of the Realm of November 15, 1869, and for the other half there shall be paid what is stipulated in article 53 of the contract now in force.

ART. 68. For the transportation of persons constituting the family of a public officer the State shall pay to the company of mail steamers as follows:

Twenty-five per cent of the transportation charges of a passage equal to that of the employee for each of his children, and 50 per cent for the legitimate wife and for the mother of said officer.

ART. 69. For the children of an employee who are under 5 years of age no transportation charges shall be paid by him to the company.

If his children are over 5 and below 10 years of age, the officer shall pay to the company from his own money for each child 25 per cent of the price of the official transportation of the same category as that which is given him personally.

If they are over 10 years of age, he shall pay to the company in the same manner 75 per cent of the transportation charges of a passage equal in amount to the charges paid for his own transportation.

For the transportation of his wife or his mother said officer shall pay 50 per cent in the same manner as specified in the preceding paragraphs.

ART. 70. The Government shall also make allowance for transportation of employees and their families transferred from one colonial province to another, or from the latter to the peninsula, in the form and to the persons specified in the preceding articles.

Officers appointed to the capitals of the Mariana and the Caroline Islands, and *vice versa*, as well as their families, are also entitled to transportation from Manila to the same, and *vice versa*, at the expense of the Government in the established form.

ART. 71. Expenses of transportation in the manner and form established in the foregoing articles shall be allowed only to the persons who have made a direct voyage in the mail steamers of the chartered company of the sea mail service.

Those who have not made a direct voyage, or if they have made it on other lines of transportation, it shall be construed in each case that they have traveled at their own expense and that they have renounced the allowance for transportation.

ART. 72. The colonial department shall publish the instructions for establishing in a definite manner the time and form in which allowance for transportation is to be made; the manner of qualifying the right to obtain the same; dates within which claims may be made and authorities to whom they should be made; nullity of that right; regulating, in addition, everything which pertains to this branch of the service of State and is related with the provisions of article 53 of the contract of the sea mail services, approved by the counsel of secretaries on November 17, 1886, ratified by the Cortes, and published June 26, 1887.

ART. 73. The periods within which public officers appointed to colonial provinces must embark shall be limited to a period of forty-five days, which can not be extended, for officers appointed to the islands of Cuba and Puerto Rico, and sixty days for those appointed to the Philippines or to the Spanish possessions of the Gulf of Guinea.

These periods shall be counted from the date of appointment.

The employees transferred from one colonial province to another, or from the latter to the peninsula, shall begin their voyage within the maximum period of sixty days, counted from the date on which the Governor-General attaches his approval to the order conferring the new office.

Those coming from the Philippines or from the Spanish possessions of the Gulf of Guinea and going to Cuba or Puerto Rico, or *vice versa*, may remain in the peninsula during the time allowed in article 54 of this decree.

ART. 74. Should any employees take time in excess of the periods allowed in the preceding article for their respective cases, they shall be declared suspended, but a new appointment may be reserved for them if opportunity presents itself.

Chapter VIII.

SUBSTITUTIONS AND TEMPORARY EMPLOYMENT.

Art. 75. Vacancies that may occur for any causes whatsoever in the service of the general administration of state of the colonial provinces, not calling for security, may be filled temporarily by substitution, according to the regulations.

For the convenience of the service in special cases, governors general may appoint to replace the chief of a dependency an officer with sufficient qualifications, serving in the branch in which the vacancy occurs, provided that he is not of the same office.

An officer has sufficient qualifications who shall be equal in category at least to a substitute appointed according to the regulations who in normal conditions would be called upon to replace the regular employee in the office in question.

Offices of superior chiefs of administration may be intrusted also to civil employees occupying a position in the category of chief of administration of the first class, without regard to the office and the branch of the service to which said position corresponds; but in such cases governors-general shall limit themselves to reporting the vacancy by telegraph to the colonial department, in order that the latter may make an appointment.

Art. 76. No substitute shall receive a salary other than that of his regular office.

In the special case provided for in the preceding article a substitute shall draw, besides the personal salary of his office, the extra pay of the office he substitutes, or the expenses of representation if the budget provides them for said office.

Governors-general may also fill provisionally other vacancies which occur in the various dependencies of the State in the respective provinces and which can not be filled by substitution according to the regulations, because professional degrees or special ability are required for their filling, by granting appointment to active or suspended officers, or, in default of such, to private individuals having the necessary qualifications, when the exigencies of the service demand such action.

In a similar manner positions which can not be substituted according to the regulations, because there is no other position in the same office, and positions which remain without employees after the filling of vacancies in the manner prescribed in article 75 may be filled temporarily with active or suspended officers or with private individuals, when such action is demanded by the considerations of benefit to the service.

In such cases of original vacancies and in cases of vacancies arising from and produced by filling other vacancies the officers concerned shall enjoy either only the extra pay or both the pay and the extra pay fixed in the budget for the office which they fill, according to whether it is vacant temporarily or actually.

Art. 78. Vacancies in offices calling for security shall be filled with officers of the active or the passive lists, who shall tender the proper security.

If a position calling for security is actually vacant, the provisional appointee shall draw the pay and the extra pay of the office he discharges; and the salary shall serve as the basis of regulating his passive qualification whenever he draws said salary for more than two years, even if not consecutively, and when he previously filled as an incumbent an office of equal category and class.

If the vacancy is temporary, the appointee shall have a right to draw only the extra pay of the office in which he replaces a regular incumbent,

ART. 79. Every temporary filling of offices of royal appointment shall be submitted for the approval of the colonial department.

ART. 80. The time spent in temporary service by suspended officers shall be taken into account in their passive classification, provided that said temporary appointment has been approved by royal order.

CHAPTER IX.

OFFENSES OF EMPLOYEES AND THEIR PUNISHMENT.

ART. 81. Offenses against discipline committed by employees of the administrative branch of the service in the colonies shall be punished by a deduction from their salary of a sum not exceeding the pay for fifteen days. Such offenses shall be decided on and punished by the chief of the respective dependency, after an oral hearing of the employee, with a right of written appeal to the higher chief of the branch, who after due investigation shall make a decision which can not be appealed from.

Five offenses against discipline shall be cause for discharge of the employee committing them.

ART. 82. Serious offenses shall be punished with suspension of pay from one to three months and with discharge from the service. A serious offense may be a cause for the immediate discharge of the employee committing it. Three suspensions of salary for serious offenses shall always result, as an inevitable consequence, in a discharge, without necessity of further proceedings.

Without prejudice to the powers conferred on chiefs of central offices and of dependencies, for disciplinary punishment of serious offenses, said offenses shall be decided on in cases in which such action is commended, by a jury composed of the superior chief of the branch, two chiefs of the dependency in which the employee renders his services, and two employees of the category immediately superior to that of the employee who committed the offense.

If in the dependency in which the offender serves the two chiefs mentioned above are lacking they shall be selected from another dependency.

ART. 83. Said jury must meet and a sentence shall be imposed upon an employee, when a public accusation is made against the latter, when said action is requested by his chiefs, when it is ordered by the governor-general, or when three judicial attachments have been decreed against the salary of that employee.

The president of the jury shall state verbally to the defendant the charges that are brought against him; and the latter shall refute the charges in the same way; and after due explanations and the evidence necessary for the decision, the defendant shall retire and the jury shall deliberate and vote by ballot with black and white balls.

If the explanations and evidence can not be obtained at once, the jury shall fix a day for pronouncing the sentence.

Discharge from the service effected in this manner shall be final.

If in the investigation thus effected there are grounds for presuming that a crime has been committed, the proceedings shall be transmitted, without loss of time, to the proper courts of justice.

ART. 84. The decisions of the jury shall always contain a statement of reasons, and a report on all of them shall be given to the colonial department. If the latter is of the opinion that the decision of the jury is not of sufficient severity, said department is at liberty to order that the delinquent officer be discharged from the service.

CHAPTER X.

REWARDS.

ART. 85. The employees of the colonial administration have a right:
1. To receive 5 per cent of the sums embezzled or taken away from the public treasury which, unknown to the administration, shall be discovered and refunded through their agency, except in the cases in which the laws in force give them a right to a greater percentage.
2. To be rewarded for their extraordinary services with honorable mention, decorations, grant of a category higher than their actual one, and pecuniary rewards granted for a time, or for life, to an amount which may reach 10 per cent of their entire personal salary. In order that the latter reward may be given, it is necessary that the service which is the object of reward be proven by proper proceedings, that it be recommended by the superior chief of the employee, and be favorably commented upon by the council of state.

CHAPTER XI.

OBLIGATIONS OF EMPLOYEES.

ART. 86. Colonial employees shall be obliged:
1. To observe irreproachable conduct in their official relations with the public and with their colleagues, and in relations of any kind with their superiors.
2. To come to the office at the assigned hours and not to leave until the chief of the dependency permits them to do so.
3. To fulfill with zeal, diligence, and eagerness all the duties intrusted to them.
4. To keep secret all matters referring to the transaction and disposal of affairs.
5. Not to practice law or act as agents for any persons on any occasion, in any place, or in any manner.

CHAPTER XII.

GENERAL PROVISIONS.

ART. 87. Every appointment made by royal decree shall be published in full in the *Gaceta de Madrid* within the period of twenty days, computed from the date on which said appointment is made.

The appointments made by royal order shall be published every fifteen days in full in the same Gaceta within the period of twenty days following the 15th and 30th of the month in which the appointments are made, stating the series of succession to which said appointments correspond.

ART. 88. Of each four vacancies of unrestricted appointment that may occur in each one of the categories and classes included in the personnel of the secretary's office of the colonial department and its dependencies of Madrid, one must indispensably be filled with an officer who serves or has served in the islands of Cuba, Puerto Rico, the

Philippines, or the Spanish possessions of the Gulf of Guinea, and who, besides possessing the legal qualifications required for the office in question, has to his credit two years of service in those provinces or possessions in an office of the same or higher category and class, deductions being made for leaves granted for Europe.

ART. 89. The provisions regulating passive rights and privileges established before the publication of the law of June 29, 1888, on colonial officers, as well as those conceded to the widows, o.phans, and mothers of said employees, are hereby preserved in full force.

An equivalent of two monthly payments of the total salary to the representatives of colonial employees dying while filling an office, as granted by base 7 of article 23 of the budget law issued for the island of Cuba for the fiscal year of 1890–91, shall be paid at once to the widow of the employee or to his children, with the condition that this sum shall be repaid in case they shall be given a pension of any kind. This repayment shall be effected by deducting 20 per cent from the monthly payments of the pension.

ART. 90. Those who belong or have belonged in the colonies to corps of militia with military organizations, volunteers of fire department, and who have to their credit six years in the service of said corps, shall be considered at the proper time as possessing the abilities, and may enjoy the privileges which the Peninsular laws grant those who serve or have served in the Army.

ART. 91. Disbursing officers and comptrollers shall, under their personal liability, refuse to pay the salary to employees whose appointment and temporary service are not made in strict compliance with the provisions of this decree-law.

ART. 92. All the laws, regulations, and provisions of a general character, in so far as they conflict with the provisions of this decree-law, are hereby repealed.

ADDITIONAL ARTICLES.

1. The provisions of this decree-law shall be observed without prejudice to the provisions of the law of July 10, 1885, and of the regulations published for its execution, in matters relating to offices reserved for sergeants of the army.

2. The appointments of superior chiefs of administration of secretaries of General Government in the colonial provinces, and of civil governors, are not subject to the series of succession established in this decree law.

TEMPORARY PROVISIONS.

1. The active and passive employees of the colonial provinces shall be subject to the qualification to be made of their ability and conduct.

2. For this purpose a qualification commission of the colonial personnel is created, which shall be composed of one ex-secretary or ex-governor-general of the island of Cuba, Puerto Rico, or the Philippines as president, and of six members, of which three shall be of the class of intendents-general of the treasury, or directors-general of the administration, who shall have been regular incumbents of said offices in the said colonies, and the remaining three of unrestricted appointment. The youngest member of the latter shall perform the duties of secretary.

3. The commission itself, in performing the duties that are intrusted to it, shall adopt such measures as are expedient for the best fulfillment of its work. All the dependencies and offices of the administrative service, both active and passive, shall be obliged to render their assistance to the commission.

Its decisions, whether excluding from or including in the graded lists any employees, shall be final, and, consequently, can not be appealed from. The commission shall not cease to perform its duties until the general graded lists are published after the qualification of employees shall have been completed.

4. The active or suspended colonial employees shall present to the commission their records of service through the chiefs of the dependencies in which they serve or served last. The chiefs shall report in said leaves of service as fully as possible, and in a confidential manner, all matters known about the record and conduct of each employee, for which purpose said chiefs shall take pains to collect, if possible, the necessary data.

5. As fast as the service records are presented they shall be examined by the commission, and the latter shall take pains, whenever it thinks such action necessary, to amplify the data and memoranda facilitating a strict examination of the personal history of each employee.

6. After the personnel has been qualified, the employees with good qualifications shall be arranged in the final graded lists of active and suspended officers in the order of seniority of each category and class. When other conditions are equal, priority shall be given to the employee who has served the longest time in the service of the State, and in case of equality even in this respect, priority shall be given to the employee of greater age.

7. Employees who do not present their records of service within the time fixed by the commission, and those who, after presenting said records, are not favorably qualified, shall not be included in the graded lists, being at once excluded from them, and shall not have a right to serve in the colonial provinces.

8. Until the provisional graded lists treated of in article 38 are published the vacancies that may occur shall be filled by the third, fourth, and fifth series of succession with active or suspended employees possessing the qualifications required by this law, without observance of the preference by right of seniority.

Given at San Sebastián, on October 13, 1890.

MARÍA CRISTINA.

ANTONIO MARIA FABIÉ,
  Secretary of the Colonies.

———

Royal decree of October 31, 1890, containing the regulations for competitive examinations for entering the judicial and public prosecution services.

In view of the reasons stated to me by the secretary of the colonies I decree the following:

ART. 1. Entrance into the judicial and the public prosecution services of the colonial provinces shall be effected through the offices of judges of the promotion category, secretaries, vice secretaries of criminal audiencias, secretaries of courts of examination, *promotores fiscales* of the promotion and the entrance categories, and shall be granted after a competitive examination.

ART. 2. The competitive examinations for filling the positions mentioned in the preceding article shall be called when demanded by the exigencies of the service, and only for the vacancies existing at the time, for both the judicial and the public prosecution services conjointly.

If the number of vacancies does not reach fifty, the examination shall be called for at least that number.

ART. 3. The competitive examinations shall be held for each call in the peninsula, Cuba, Puerto Rico, and the Philippines.

ART. 4. A call for competitive examinations shall be made by the colonial secretary by communicating the proper orders to the general direction of grace and justice of the department and to the respective governors-general of the colonial possessions, and shall be published in the official gacetas.

ART. 5. In filling each fifty vacancies thirty appointments shall be given to peninsular competitors, ten to those of Cuba, five to those of Puerto Rico, and five to those of the Philippines, all the remaining vacancies being distributed in the same manner and proportion.

ART. 6. The periods assigned for presenting petitions for admission to examinations shall be forty-five days for those to be held in the peninsula, and thirty days for those to be held in the Antilles or in the Phillippines, computed from the day following the publication of the call in the respective official gacetas.

ART. 7. In order to be admitted to a competitive examination, a candidate must be a Spaniard, a layman, a licentiate at law from a university subsidized by the State, and must be at least 23 years of age before the day on which the examination exercises begin.

There can not be admitted to the examination:

First. Those physically or mentally unsound.

Second. Those prosecuted for any crime.

Third. Those condemned to any correctional or corporeal punishment.

Fourth. Those who have suffered or undergone a penalty which lowers them in the public esteem.

Fifth. Those who have been discharged provisionally from a criminal prosecution, when they are considered innocent through the lapse of time.

Sixth. Bankrupts who have not been discharged.

Seventh. Insolvent debtors until they are declared freed from debts.

Eighth. Debtors to public funds, as taxpayers.

Ninth. Those who have committed acts and omissions which, though not penal, lower them in the public esteem.

ART. 8. Persons desiring to enter the judicial or the public prosecution services shall accredit to the direction of grace and justice, or to the respective governors general, as the case may be, according as to whether the examinations are to be held in the Peninsula or in the colonies, the qualifications stated in the first part of the preceding article.

Proceedings shall be instituted for each candidate.

The lists of the persons admitted to an examination shall be published in the respective official Gacetas.

ART. 9. The examiners' board for examinations held in the Peninsula shall be composed of the following persons:

The presiding judge of the supreme court, who shall be the president of the board.

The *fiscal* of the supreme court.

Two associate justices of the same court, or of the audiencia of Madrid, appointed by the secretary of the colonies.

The dean of the bar of Madrid.

A lawyer appointed by the secretary of the colonies from among those who pay as such, one of the first three quotas of the industrial subsidy.

A professor of law at the Central University, appointed by the secretary of the colonies.

And one lawyer as secretary, with the right of vote, appointed by the secretary of the colonies.

ART. 10. The examiners' board for examinations to be held in Cuba, Puerto Rico, or the Philippines shall be composed of:

The presiding judge of the audiencia of Habana, Puerto Rico, or Manila, who shall be the president of the respective board.

The *fiscal* of the corresponding audiencia.

One associate justice of an audiencia, appointed by the respective governor-general.

One professor of a university, or an institute, who is a lawyer, appointed by the governor-general.

One councilor of administration, lawyer, or one associate justice of the court of administrative litigation, appointed by the governor-general.

One lawyer appointed by the said governor-general.

One lawyer, as secretary, with a right of vote, appointed by the governor-general.

ART. 11. The members of the examining board other than ex-officio, shall cease to be such when new examinations are held, unless they are reelected.

ART. 12. In cases when the presiding judge or the *fiscal* of the supreme court, the presiding judge or the *fiscal* of the audiencia in question, or the dean of the bar can not attend the examiners' board on account of incompatibility or any other cause, they shall be substituted as follows:

The presiding judge of the supreme court or of the audiencia, by the presiding judge of chamber of the respective court, appointed by the department or by the governor-general, in a proper case.

The *fiscal* of the supreme court, or of the audiencia by the *teniente fiscal* of the same court, and, in his default, by one of the *abogados fiscales* designated by the department or by the respective governor-general.

The dean of the bar by a member of its administrative board, appointed in the same manner.

ART. 13. The list of the competitors admitted to examinations shall be transmitted to the proper court with the proceedings that have taken place.

ART. 14. The appointment of the board judging examinations shall be announced in the official papers on the same day on which the call for the examination is published.

The court shall publish a programme of the examinations within twenty days following said publication. The programme shall also be inserted in the proper official *Gaceta*, and shall include at least 100 questions on each course of lectures in the civil, commercial, and penal laws and the civil and the criminal procedures; 25 questions on each of the courses in the political, administrative, canonical and ecclesiastical disciplinary laws, and 15 questions each on the mortgage, notarial, and civil registry laws.

ART. 15. Before the examinations have begun, the competitors shall be numbered by publicly drawing lots. The person who does not present himself when called for the examination in the order of numbers obtained in drawing lots shall be called the second time after the last one on the list, and if he does not present himself the second time he shall lose his right to take part in the examinations.

Art. 16. The examinations shall be public. The first exercise shall be oral and the second written.

Art. 17. The first exercise shall consist in answering, without previous preparation, fifteen questions drawn by lot in the following proportion:

Two questions in the civil law, two in the penal law, two in the commercial law, two in the civil and criminal procedures, and one for each of the remaining subjects mer tioned in article 14.

The time for answering these questions can not exceed one hour and a half.

Art. 18. The second examination shall consist of a compilation of a sentence, resolution, or accusation, in a civil or a criminal matter, as designated by drawing lots.

In order to prepare this work the presidents of the boards shall request of the presiding judges of the respective audiencias a number of proceedings equal to double the number of competitors.

These proceedings, properly modified so as to conceal the part of the work of which the examination shall consist, shall be preserved by the president of the board with the utmost secrecy.

To draft a resolution, accusation, or sentence, of which the exercise shall consist, the competitors shall be separated in rooms designated for the purpose, shall have at their disposal four hours of preparation, and shall be given the legal texts which they may request.

After the four hours have elapsed the competitors must deliver their work in folded sheets in a sealed and signed envelope. When the board convenes each competitor shall open his envelope, read his work, and, after reading the same, shall leave it at the disposal of the president.

Art. 19. At the end of the exercises of each day the board shall immediately, in a secret vote, qualify the work of competitors by using one of the following marks: "Approved" or "Suspended," and shall post the result of this qualification on the door of the room in which the exercises are held. After the completion of all of the exercises the court, in a secret vote, shall qualify the competitors in the numerical order based on their relative merit, and shall submit its recommendation to the secretary of the colonies.

Under no consideration can the number of places announced in a call for an examination be increased. The courts shall abstain from including in their recommendations a number of competitors larger than the number of places for which the examination has been held.

Art. 20. After an examination has ended, the lists and proceedings of each competitor shall be sent to the secretary of the colonies, who shall make appointments from among the approved competitors with the observance of the numerical order in which they are arranged by the board of examiners, and in conformity with the provisions of the articles that follow.

Art. 21. When recommendations of competitors have been received at the department, a graded list of the candidates shall be arranged and published in the official gacetas, subject to the following rules:

The graded list shall begin with the names of the competitors from the Peninsula who occupy the first three numbers on the list; these shall be followed by the names of the candidates who obtained the first number in Cuba, Puerto Rico, and the Philippines, successively, and the same order and proportion shall be observed in the remaining part of the list until the end of the recommendation.

Art. 22. Inferior courts of the entrance category and other positions of the same category which are vacant at the present time, or which may hereafter become vacant, shall be filled in conformity with the following series of succession:

For the first vacancy appointment shall be made of the candidate who has the lowest number in the graded list of his class.

For the second vacancy appointment shall be made of the *promotor* of the entrance category of the greatest seniority who has one year to his credit in that category.

For the third vacancy appointment shall be made of a suspended officer of the same category who has solicited appointment.

In default of *promotores* and suspended officers, appointment shall be made of the competitor whose number corresponds to the appointment.

ART. 23. Offices of *promotores* of the entrance category which are now vacant or may become vacant hereafter shall be filled in accordance with the following series of succession:

For the first and second vacancy appointment shall be made of a competitor whose number corresponds to said appointment.

For the third vacancy appointment shall be made of a suspended officer who has solicited appointment or of a competitor whose number corresponds to said appointment.

ART. 24. Offices of judges of the entrance category and their equals, and offices of *promotores* of the entrance category which are vacant at the time of the publication of this decree law, or which may hereafter become vacant, shall be distributed in the following manner:

The former shall be awarded to the competitors occupying the first numbers in the graded list, according to strict order, and in conformity with the provisions of article 19; and the latter shall be awarded to the remaining competitors in the same form and in conformity with the provisions of the preceding article.

ART. 25. Competitors appointed to the Antilles or to the Philippines may accept or refuse the office conferred on them until there occur vacancies of the category in that of the two territories mentioned above which they may prefer.

Those offered appointment as *promotores* of the entrance category may also either accept or refuse the appointment until there occurs a vacancy of the rank of judge of the entrance category, for which vacancy, as in the preceding case, preference shall be given to the competitor who holds a lower number on the graded list.

The privileges given in this article shall be limited to the date of filling of the last position accepted by the appointees voluntarily; and it shall be construed that the candidate who renounces the service, after being appointed the second time in the proper order, does not accept the office for which he has been designated.

ART. 26. The royal decrees of October 26, 1888, and of March 15, 1889, and the royal order of August 8, of the same year, are hereby repealed in so far as they refer to entrance into the judicial and the public prosecution service.

Given at the Palace October 31, 1890.

MARÍA CRISTIANA.

ANTONIO MARÍA FABIÉ,
Secretary of the Colonies.

Alphabetical list of the inferior courts of Cuba, Puerto Rico, and the Philippines, with a statement of their category and audiencia to which each of them belongs.

Inferior court.	Category.	Audiencia to which it belongs.
Abra	Entrance	Manila.
Aguadilla	....do	Mayagüez.
Albay	Final	Manila.
Alfonso XII	Entrance	Matanzas.
Antique	....do	Cebú.
Arecibo	Promotion	Mayagüez.
Audiencia of Habana (first instance)	Associate justice of the territorial audiencia.	Habana.
Baracoa	Entrance	Santiago de Cuba.
Barotac Viejo	....do	Cebú.
Bataan	Final	Manila.
Batanes Islands	Entrance	Do.
Batangas	Final	Do.
Bayamo	Entrance	Santiago de Cuba.
Bejucal	....do	Habana.
Binondo de Manila	Final	Manila.
Bohol	Entrance	Cebú.
Bulacán	Final	Manila.
Cagayán	Entrance	Do.
Calamianes	....do	Cebú.
Camarines Norte	Promotion	Manila.
Camarines Sur	....do	Do.
Cápiz	Entrance	Cebú.
Cárdenas	Promotion	Matanzas.
Cavite	Entrance	Manila.
Cayey	....do	San Juan de Puerto Rico.
Cebú	Promotion	Cebú.
Central, of Habana (examination)	Associate justice of the territorial audiencia.	Habana.
Central, of Habana (first instance)	....do	Do.
Cienfuegos	Promotion	Santa Clara
Coamo	Entrance	Ponce.
Colón	....do	Matanzas.
East of Habana (examination)	Associate justice of the territorial audiencia.	Habana.
East of Habana (first instance)	....do	Do.
Guanabacoa	Entrance	Do.
Guanajay	....do	Pinar del Río.
Guane	....do	Do.
Guantánamo	....do	Santiago de Cuba.
Guayama	....do	Ponce.
Güines	....do	Habana.
Habana. (*See* Audiencia, Central, East, and West of same.)		
Holguín	....do	Santiago de Cuba.
Humacao	....do	San Juan de Puerto Rico.
Ilo Ilo	Promotion	Cebú.
Ilocos Norte	Final	Manila.
Ilocos Sur	....do	Do.
Intramuros, of Manila	....do	Do.
Isabela (La)	Entrance	Do.
Island of Negros	....do	Cebú.
Islands, Batanes	....do	Manila.
Islands, Ladrones (Marianas)	....do	Do.
Jaruco	....do	Habana.
Ladrones Islands	....do	Manila.
Laguna	Final	Do.
La Isabela	Entrance	Do.
Leyte	....do	Cebú.
Manila. (*See* Binondo, Intramuros, Quiapo, and Tondo de Manila.)		
Manzanillo	....do	Santiago de Cuba.
Marianao	....do	Habana.
Marianas Islands	....do	Manila.
Matanzas. (*See* North of Matanzas, and South of Matanzas.)		
Mayagüez	Promotion	Mayagüez.
Mindoro	....do	Manila.
Misamis	Entrance	Cebú.
Morón	....do	Puerto Príncipe.
Negros Island	....do	Cebú.
Negros Island	....do	Do.
North of Matanzas	Promotion	Matanzas.
North of Santiago de Cuba	Final	Santiago de Cuba.
Nueva Ecija	Promotion	Manila.
Nueva Vizcaya	Entrance	Do.
Oeste. (*See* West.)		
Pampanga	Final	Do.
Pangasinam	....do	Do.
Pinar del Río	Promotion	Pinar del Río.